CLOAK WITHOUT DAGGER

CLOAK
WITHOUT DAGGER

by

SIR PERCY SILLITOE
K.B.E.

CASSELL AND COMPANY LTD
LONDON

CASSELL & CO LTD
37/38 St. Andrew's Hill, Queen Victoria Street,
London, E.C.4

and at

31–34 George IV Bridge, Edinburgh
210 Queen Street, Melbourne
26–30 Clarence Street, Sydney
Uhlmann Road, Hawthorne, Brisbane
C.P.O. 3031, Auckland, N.Z.
1068 Broadview Avenue, Toronto 6
P.O. Box 275, Cape Town
P.O. Box 1386, Salisbury, S. Rhodesia
Munsoor Building, Main Street, Colombo 11
Haroon Chambers, South Napier Road, Karachi
13–14 Ajmeri Gate Extention, New Delhi 1
15 Graham Road, Ballard Estate, Bombay 1
17 Chittaranjan Avenue, Calcutta 13
Avenida 9 de Julho 1138, São Paulo
Galeria Güemes, Escritorio 518–520 Florida 165, Buenos Aires
P.O. Box 959, Accra, Gold Coast
25 rue Henri Barbusse, Paris 5e
Islands Brygge 5, Copenhagen

SET IN 12 PT. BEMBO TYPE AND
PRINTED IN GREAT BRITAIN
BY EBENEZER BAYLIS AND SON, LTD., THE
TRINITY PRESS, WORCESTER, AND LONDON
F.155

FOREWORD

by

The Rt. Hon. C. R. ATTLEE,

P.C., O.M., C.H., M.P.

A Director-General of M.I.5 needs very special qualities. He has to have the technical qualities required for intelligence work. He must be able to control a team of individualists engaged on important secret work. At the same time he has to have a very lively appreciation of the rights of the citizen in a free country.

M.I.5, though technically a branch of the War Office, is under the direct control of the Prime Minister. He can only perform his duty in this regard by selecting for the topmost the right man, a man on whom he can rely with complete confidence. When it fell to me to make this appointment, I was fortunate in finding Sir Percy Sillitoe.

This straightforward biography reveals very clearly the manner of man he is and why he was so successful. The reader will find much of absorbing interest, but is sure to wish that the obligations of secrecy had not prevented Sir Percy from lifting the veil from his activities in his last post.

He has told his life story from the time when he was a chorister in St. Paul's Cathedral Choir until he retired full of honours and vigour. On the way he recounts his adventurous career in wild Africa and his services as a Chief Constable at home.

In a world where so many millions groan under the tyranny of the Police State, it is good to read the life of a man who exhibits the qualities which have made the British policeman the protector not the oppressor of society.

CONTENTS

ILLUSTRATIONS

INTRODUCTION

A PREDILECTION for law and order is common to all policemen and I, being no exception, have liked to consider my own life as a reasonably well-ordered affair. It is for that reason, perhaps, that I wish I could persuade myself that my appointment as Director-General of M.I.5 fulfilled my life's ambition and was the goal towards which I had always striven. Surely, a well-ordered career should culminate in a long-desired success! But, though I am probably as ambitious as the next man, I had never in any complacent daydream visualized myself at the head of M.I.5. The post was not, I think, one to which the aspirations of a policeman would normally have turned.

It was in November 1945 that I received from Sir Alexander Maxwell, then Permanent Under-Secretary of State for the Home Department, a letter asking if I would allow myself to be considered as a candidate for the post of Director-General of the British Security Service. At this time William Joyce had just been brought to trial and public concern about the harm which can be done to a nation by a handful of traitors in its midst was acute. Yet, in a sense, it was retrospective alarm, for the war was over and few people were giving thought to the necessity for warding off threats from any direction other than Germany. Already, however, details of Russian espionage in Canada had been revealed to the Canadian Government by a Soviet Embassy cipher clerk who had decided to throw in his lot with the democracies. Alan Nunn May had returned to this country after unlawfully divulging information on atomic energy research, on which he himself had been working in Montreal. Klaus Fuchs had for some time been handing over information to a Russian agent: information which had included precise details of the atomic bomb. These facts were as yet unknown to the public, but they were the seeds of the events which were to be the most spectacular during my term of office at M.I.5, and they were already sown.

Since 1943, I myself had been Chief Constable of Kent County Police, and I had felt no inclination to change my job. However, I was naturally gratified to realize I might be offered this appointment of unique interest and unusual responsibility. On the other hand, the prospect suddenly before me caused me qualms that would not have been occasioned by the offer of any straightforward police work. I should have felt immediately confident of undertaking this efficiently. I should have had a fairly precise conception of its duties and the problems to be faced; I should have known the sort of men I should be dealing with and I should have been forewarned of pitfalls and guided in decisions by long years of practical experience.

I had no way of gauging my potential ability to direct the Security Service. In common with the vast majority of the public, I knew very little of the work of M.I.5, and virtually nothing of the duties of its chief. Like most people, I had suffered pangs of frustrated curiosity about its successful operations of which no details were ever published, and had felt unsympathetic indignation at its alleged failures which, inevitably, had become news in my daily newspaper. I had occasionally succumbed to the temptation which almost everyone finds irresistible—that of making fun of the "cloak and dagger boys" whom one imagines as heavy-handed British blimps, making ludicrously melodramatic and totally unconvincing efforts to outwit subtle and unfathomable foreigners.

Thinking more seriously, I knew, of course, that the Security Service was responsible for collecting information about people who intend to subvert British institutions and also for devising ways and means of countering their activities. The Department's job is to identify the enemy, to find out what he is doing and by what methods he is working; then to pursue and neutralize him.

I also realized that often when M.I.5 came in for criticism and people asked heatedly why the Department did not "do something" in an affair where there seemed to be grounds for suspicion if nothing else, the public—and the Press also—were forgetting that the Security Service has no executive responsibility. It can only submit information and evidence which, if it is deemed incriminating by the Director of Public Prosecutions, will result in a warrant for arrest being issued, or, perhaps, in an intimation to some foreign embassy that a certain member of the embassy staff is no longer *persona grata* in this country. But—fortunately—in Britain there can be no issue of a warrant for anyone's arrest unless there is sufficient legal evidence available to justify it, and often intelligence information does not constitute legal evidence. Often, too, it would be imprudent to produce such information if that were to mean that its implications and the method by which it was acquired were revealed, for usually intelligence information does not relate only to isolated acts, but has a bearing on many other matters of far-reaching importance whose ramifications are most intricately entwined. In cases of espionage, as Mr. J. Edgar Hoover, head of the Federal Bureau of Investigation in the United States, pointed out at a rather later period, "arrest and public disclosure are steps to be taken only as a matter of last resort. It is better to know who these people are and what they are doing, and to immobilize their efforts, than it is to expose them publicly and then go through the tireless efforts of identifying their successors." My appreciation of this feature of M.I.5's activities, and also my realization of the hazy and short-sighted nature of public criticism, were both to grow more vivid in the years to come.

When eventually I was summoned for an interview, I was asked what I knew about M.I.5. I had to admit that my knowledge of its functions was very sparse indeed. However, I suppose I was in no worse a state of ignorance than was expected. At all events, a few months later I was appointed by the Prime Minister, then Mr. Attlee, as Director-General, and when I took up this appointment—on 1st May 1946, the day on which Alan Nunn May was charged at the Old Bailey with communicating information contrary to the Official Secrets Act—I had to some extent assessed the problems that lay ahead of me. I realized that I had a big job and heavy responsibilities, but I thought I could tackle them adequately with common sense and energy, a fresh outlook on old obstacles and an enterprising approach to new problems.

Among the points that were called especially to my attention was the ruling that the work of M.I.5 is unconnected with political matters, and that it must never be thought or suggested that the politics of those who seek to subvert our realm or institutions have a bearing on M.I.5's activities to frustrate their efforts. It so happened that this admonition acquired a great significance during my period of office. For the "cold war" has led many people to regard M.I.5 as a militant organization entrusted with the task of waging an underground battle against the Communists and in particular the U.S.S.R. It must be borne in mind that the function of M.I.5 is purely a defensive one; it is charged solely with detecting activities liable to undermine the national security of this country; and the creed, politics, or nationalities of those responsible for such activities is immaterial. It has no authority to take any measures that are not directly aimed at the prevention or frustration of attempts to undermine our safety and endanger this realm.

With the opening of, as it were, a new phase of espionage marked by the disclosures made by Gouzenko, the Soviet Embassy cipher clerk who first revealed the extent of Russian espionage in Canada, the security arrangements of countries in the British Commonwealth apart from the United Kingdom became a matter of great concern to M.I.5. Previously the dominions had been regarded as reasonably immune from subversive activities, but now that they were vitally concerned in co-operating with the United Kingdom in defence measures and in scientific research to protect our common interests, it was obvious that they had become a fruitful field for espionage. So far as the colonies were concerned, Stalin had, in effect, recommended to the Communist Press that it should prepare the minds of colonial peoples for revolt, and his dictum had already been followed by an immense increase in the flow of Communist propaganda to the British colonies.

As a result of the spread of international espionage to parts of the Commonwealth outside the United Kingdom, I was to become the first chief of M.I.5 to travel extensively during my term of office. I had been well acquainted with Northern and Southern Rhodesia and Tanganyika Territory in my youth,

for, at the age of twenty, I was serving in the British South
Africa Police, and I had remained in Africa for close on fifteen
years. But between 1946 and my retirement in 1953 I was invited to visit not only Africa and Canada, where I discussed
our common security problems, but also Australia, New Zealand, and Malaya, where I was able to advise on the spot about
the setting up or the improvement of security organizations.
My high opinion of security arrangements throughout the
Commonwealth now is therefore wedded to keen personal
interest in the problems and the achievements of the Commonwealth organizations.

Although it seemed at first that work at M.I.5 was to be a
completely new departure for me, I soon found that my earlier
experience was standing me in good stead. While I was putting
the value of that experience to the test, I often cast my mind
back over the problems and excitements of my earlier years.
And then, eventually, when the time came for me to think of
retirement, I wondered if the kind people who had assured me
my adventures would "read like a book" were perhaps to be
taken seriously.

CHAPTER ONE

Schooldays at St. Paul's – My first job – I join the British South Africa Police and sail for Southern Rhodesia.

To begin, then, at the beginning. My father was a man who always impressed people with his great personal charm. He had, besides, an excellent head for figures. From Shropshire, where our family had lived for generations, he came to London when he was twenty, with a certain amount of money; and, by investing with bold assurance, he began to prosper.

Unfortunately this early success proved to be his undoing, for he was not richly endowed with business sense. I had been born at Tulse Hill in London in 1888, and by the time my elder brother, Hubert, and I were at an age to be sent to a prep school the family budget had ceased to balance. The immediate cause was that my father had invested every penny he possessed in Mexican Rails. Some years afterwards these shares were to rise phenomenally, and make large fortunes for investors. But, like most shares, these ones were a thought capricious, and before they rose they first descended, and while they were in the doldrums my father sold ours for practically nothing. It is not for me to be wise after the event and I do not really know whether it was panic or pure necessity that led him to make this mistake.

In any case, the reversal of his fortunes did not depress him. He merely remarked with some justice that as he was now penniless there was probably no future for him in the stock market. And then he found a job as an average-adjuster. This gave him pleasurable opportunities for displaying his arithmetical bent and led to his making friends whose company he enjoyed. It also provided a livelihood of a sort. But it never at any time looked like paying for the education of his two sons at a public school.

It was a lucky chance that my mother had a cousin whose father held a Governorship at Christ's Hospital, for he was able to award a presentation to my brother Hubert. This meant that, if he so wished, he could take Holy Orders. That is, in fact, what happened, and my brother Hubert is to-day Rector of Digswell in Hertfordshire. The education of my sister, Bertha, who was ten years younger than I, did not yet worry my parents unduly, but my own schooling remained an un-solved problem. With my elder brother at Christ's Hospital, my parents were reluctant to send me to a day-school, although my father could certainly afford no better. My mother, a woman of quiet determination, cudgelled her brains to find a solution and eventually did so.

I had been blessed with a good singing voice, and as my father also sang well and my mother was an exceptionally good pianist, we frequently amused ourselves with musical evenings. In this pleasant, unorganized way I was taught to sing a true note, and this small talent which we had none of us regarded as more than a casual social grace won me the good education my mother had set her heart upon, for choristers were needed at St. Paul's, and all boys who sing in the choir are taken as pupils at the Cathedral Choir School—a boarding school of accepted public preparatory school standard. One may be said to sing for one's schooling.

The acceptance tests have always been of a very high stan-dard and it has always been regarded as quite a musical distinc-tion to enter the Choir School. But when I attended the au-dition held by the organist, Sir George Martin—a straight and dapper little man with a formidable ginger beard—I was really unaware of how much my success would mean to me, and so I sang quite unselfconsciously, as I had always done at home before my parents and their guests. I had always enjoyed singing and I sang as happily for Sir George Martin as ever I had before.

As a result, Percy Joseph Sillitoe entered the Choir School at St. Paul's in 1898, and for four years sang at all the services. I can still remember vividly the wonderful scenes we boys saw from that vantage-point of considerable privilege—the choir-stalls. I was there in 1901, in the January of which year Queen Victoria died, and sang for Her Majesty's memorial service, and again for the Coronation Service of King Edward VII. I remember how we had dressed with anxious care, and stood rustling in our surplices, when the black-bearded Duke of Norfolk came in at a dress rehearsal at Westminster Abbey to announce that the Coronation was to be postponed owing to His Majesty's acute appendicitis; and I still have my ticket of entrance and copies of the music for the Coronation Service which was held eventually after the King recovered his health. My memories of the scene are still with me, also: the winking, fabulous jewels of the Eastern Potentates who to our eyes looked oddly like a particularly praiseworthy collection of Christmas trees; the unexpectedly guttural German accent of the King as he took the oath, and our pride in hearing the King's voice so close to us.

These were special occasions, but each day of every week we sang at two services, except on Sundays when there were three, and Thursdays when we were given an afternoon off which was assigned to outdoor sports. I loved the services and sang with all my heart to the angel depicted on a beautiful stained glass window above the High Altar. I returned to the Cathedral not long ago, and noticed that my angel had been mercifully spared during the bombing. But the passing years have perhaps dimmed my sight, for she did not have quite the magic I remembered. In those days of my youth she was my personal guardian angel and looked down on me with great benevolence. But now, I fear, she is merely a superb stained-glass window.

To the choristers, the eminent Churchmen of that day were familiar everyday figures, each with his own hobby-horse and his own idiosyncrasies which we accepted with the amiable tolerance schoolboys usually extend to their masters. The Dean of St. Paul's was the Very Rev. Robert Gregory, at that time a robust and vigorous old man of nearly eighty, with a some-what cumbersome body and an unwavering devotion to St.

Paul's. He did not preach often and I do not think that he could have been considered an eloquent preacher. But he would stand for no nonsense and, in his view, any opinion that did not concur with his own was nonsense; such was his air of venerable authority that no one in his congregations would ever have dreamed of challenging or even questioning his forthright pronouncements, and certainly the choristers accepted his mildest observations as gospel. The greatest orator of the Chapter was generally recognized to be Canon Henry Scott Holland, though he preached not, I am sure, with conscious rhetoric, but out of a depth of the most passionate sincerity.

The man who always filled the cathedral, however, was Winnington Ingram, Bishop of Stepney, who later became a most famous Bishop of London. He it was who succeeded in combining the human touch with a most fascinating and persuasive eloquence. On the other hand, Dr. William Sinclair, Archdeacon of London, who preached with a voice of such extraordinary resonance that he would, I know, have scorned the aid of a microphone, stirred one's imagination by his vocal talent, but somehow never captured one's attention. After a few minutes of pleasure gained from the mere sound of that remarkable voice, my mind used to wander and neither the teachings nor the exhortations of the Archdeacon influenced me in any way. Indirectly, however, this man was to shape my career, though I doubt if he ever realized that he had done so.

I do not know how the standard of preaching in those days compares with that of the present day. Churches were better attended then, but I daresay the sermons were not exclusively responsible for that. I do feel sure, however, that the prowess of organists has grown. In those days Sir George Martin performed with faultless technique, no doubt, but his playing was never memorable, while the sub-organist, Charles McPherson, who also had great technical skill, treated his instrument with a disappointing lack of imagination. The only time I fully appreciated the great organ was on one Sunday when Stanley Marchant, as guest organist, played, at the end of the service, instead of the usual medley of unintelligible extempore composition to which so many church organists are addicted, Rachmaninoff's Prelude in C Sharp Minor. This performance made me hear as if for the first time the glorious resonant tone of the notes from those great thirty-two-foot pedal pipes in the quarter-domes and it filled me with joyous amazement. It was, perhaps, the pedestrian talent of the normal run of organists that was responsible for my later heretical love of the cinema organ which remains constant to this day.

The Choir School was the responsibility of Minor Canon Morgan-Brown, an ascetic and scholarly man who discharged his duties impeccably and was highly respected. My relationships with other masters were not, however, entirely happy; probably this was through no fault of theirs, but at the time I found it difficult to recognize that. My principal misfortune during my first days at school was undoubtedly my surname, which has continued throughout my life to provoke my acquaintances to great feats of wit which, not unnaturally, have been appreciated less by me than by themselves. My schoolmasters, having a boyish sense of humour, singled me out for quips and sarcasms, for no better reason—as far as I know—than that I was called Sillitoe. To-day I am not ungrateful to them, for they soon taught me to control my temper and sit stoically and with an appearance of unconcern in the face of taunts and mockery. And since then I have always been able to risk ridicule with equanimity, so that I have not been unduly hampered in my actions by fear of derision or sarcastic criticism. It was certainly desirable that I should learn this lesson early and it has continued to stand me in good stead.

My scholarly acquaintances in my later life have also been fascinated by my name, and I have therefore accumulated from various sources quite a store of information about it. It was recorded in Yorkshire as "Selito" in 1379 when a poll tax of one to twenty shillings was imposed upon every person above the age of fifteen years—the Selitos not excluded. Eighteen years later it was rendered as "Shelito", and in other counties— Staffordshire, Cheshire, and Shropshire—other variants have been recorded. It is generally thought that its origins were Scandinavian, but I do not know exactly what reasons there are for this theory. A studious old lady bearing the same name—a distant relative of mine as it turned out—insisted with unshakable conviction that the Selitos were descended from the Vandal Stilicho who came near to seizing the Roman Empire —but I, as an ardent upholder of the law, decline to believe I am a descendant of this arrogant law-breaker.

My own family can be traced back to a John Selito of Shropshire, who was born in 1615. It was his grandson, William, who elected, when signing his will, to spell his name in the manner to which I am accustomed. Just to show that we, too, can appreciate a good pun, our family motto is: "Selito Teneto Si Leto"—which I translate inelegantly as "See it through!" and which I have always considered a most enspiriting exhortation.

Returning to my strictly disciplined schooldays, I must admit that I was not always a docile pupil. Indeed, between one master, Mr. Dowell, and myself there grew up a most unseemly feud which probably caused him great annoyance and which contributed largely to the sorry fact that I never became a remarkable scholar. I think that I was not entirely to blame for the ill-will between us. The headmaster, at the end of one term, had invited us to apply ourselves to the study of Latin and Greek during the holidays, since he considered our progress unsatisfactory. As an incentive, he promised that any boy who passed the examination he planned to set us at the beginning of the following term would be advanced to a higher form. For some reason this idea captured my imagination and during those holidays I worked with quite unusual application. I duly passed the examination and awaited my reward. But Mr. Dowell—no doubt with my scholastic interests at heart—persuaded the headmaster that I was not sufficiently advanced in other subjects to merit my promotion, and as a result I remained where I was. Such was my penetrating sense of the injustice of this procedure, that I downed tools, as it were. When Mr. Dowell became aware of my reaction I was called to be caned. He went to his cane-cupboard, produced the implement, and turned to me. And he met what must have been the most ferocious glare of his tutorial experience, for I can clearly remember how he hesitated and then said: "Sillitoe, you have the look of the very devil in your eyes. You had best return to your place." I was not caned on that occasion.

Yet, for the headmaster's brother, Mr. Heathcote Morgan-Brown, who came occasionally to the school to assist in the instruction, I was a well-behaved and enthusiastic pupil, for he was a man I greatly respected. I do not think it impossible that, if he, and not Mr. Dowell, had been my form master, I might have led a more scholarly life. As it was, apart from playing in both football and cricket teams, the only outstanding achievement that I performed at St. Paul's was winning the half-mile handicap from scratch—a feat that had never been accomplished before. Some years ago I presented a silver trophy to the School for the half-mile handicap—a memorial to my solitary success.

Notwithstanding my bad behaviour, I was allowed, along with the other boys, to accept the traditional invitations of the Canons, who lived in Amen Court, to breakfast on Sunday mornings. Nowadays I believe that this custom has lapsed and an invitation to tea has been substituted. However, in those days we went to breakfast, and we breakfasted with great relish.

It was at one of these morning feasts that my host, Dr. Sinclair, played his unwitting part in fashioning my life by introducing me to his brother—Colonel Hugh Sinclair—a fine-looking man with a straightforward manner which I found immediately sympathetic. He was just off to the Boer War. I do not remember precisely what conversation passed between us, but I know that while the sermon was being preached from the pulpit of St. Paul's that day, and on many days afterwards, a lanky choirboy was, in imagination, hunting elephant and discovering hidden gold and annihilating whole battalions of Boers at the side of Colonel Sinclair. And when the City Imperial Volunteers returned from the war and came to a Thanksgiving Service for their return, I could not take my eyes from the spears and assegais they had brought back as mementoes of their valour.

Soon after this, at the end of 1902, my singing voice was gone, and I had therefore to leave St. Paul's. My ambition was to seek adventure overseas, but I was only fourteen and my parents judged this to be an age more suitable to further schooling. However, my father's financial embarrassment was as heavy as ever and it was still impossible to send me to a public school. An ingenious solution to the problem was arrived at: I should study for the Indian Police examination at home under a tutor, thus encouraging me in my ambition to travel, while at the same time ensuring that my education was not left in too elementary a stage—and, incidentally, dispensing with school fees!

For three years I worked as best I could and read travel books about India, Africa and China in my spare time. But solitary study is difficult to sustain, especially for a young boy with no special intellectual brilliance. I was not happy with the progress I was making, and I began to suspect that it was going to be a long time before I passed the Indian Police examination. My hopes of getting to India—or indeed anywhere else—were growing horribly faint, when on my seventeenth birthday I received a letter from Colonel Sinclair. As a consequence I went to stay with him at Woolwich where he was A.Q.M.G. I lived for a while in an atmosphere of Army reminiscences, soldiers, horses and good humour, and I learned to ride polo ponies. And I decided that I had finished my studies.

The upshot of this was that I obtained, with Colonel Sinclair's assistance, a job with the Anglo-American Oil Company, with the promise that when I was twenty-one I should be sent to a foreign station, probably Japan. However, two years later, an ex-St. Paul's boy who was Secretary for Native Affairs in North-eastern Rhodesia came on leave and invited me to lunch. I returned home to announce to my mother that I was signing on for three years as a trooper in the British South Africa Police, my friend promising me an opening in North-eastern Rhodesia at the end of my service.

My mother resignedly looked up North-eastern Rhodesia in the gazetteer and found with relief that it was described as "enjoying a climate suitable for Europeans". She also found that of Southern Rhodesia it was said: "In the swamp areas around the valleys, malaria and sleeping-sickness prevail."

"I do hope that it *will* be North-eastern Rhodesia soon," she murmured.

Three weeks later I set sail with instructions to report to the recruit training centre at Salisbury—Southern Rhodesia.

CHAPTER TWO

A police trooper in Southern Rhodesia – My first man-hunt – A journey with a lunatic and an unsought adventure with a lion – Promotion – I receive my commission and join the North Rhodesia Police.

SOUTHERN Rhodesia was a wild country in those days, with few roads, and those little more than wagon tracks. All our patrolling was done on horses or mules, with pack-donkeys. Salisbury, the capital, was then a little township largely consisting of wooden houses with corrugated iron roofs. The police camp was where it is to-day, about two miles out of the town, and to reach it we had to walk across open veldt.

The recruits were a fascinating assortment: ex-public school boys, remittance men, and adventurers. The discipline was severe. One man was sentenced by the O.C. to fourteen days hard labour in the Bulawayo civil gaol, for no greater offence than that he was observed to be still slightly fuddled when reporting for duty on transfer to an outstation the morning after a canteen party. One of the inflexible rules of the British South Africa Police was never to be drunk on duty.

In such a country it was essential that police troopers should be good horsemen, and I was fortunate in having been taught to ride well by Colonel Sinclair. Some of the horses were only partly broken, and the training ground was out in the open—a real "rough-riding" school. Often—too often, I thought—the order was "cross your stirrups", an exhausting procedure to recruits and, indeed, when one had spurs on, a dangerous one too. But I suppose that, in view of the fairly recent Boer War, such exercises on the veldt were not frivolous.

Frequently the horses would break away and gallop off into the veldt with their inexperienced riders, at some risk to the latters' lives. However, there was rarely any sympathy to be expected from the instructor. "Hi! You're not followin' father's 'ounds now, you know!" he would bellow after the reluctant runaway. Then he would shade his eyes. "Watch where he settles!" he would roar, and somebody would be despatched at a gallop to pick up the discarded rider. Once a horse bolted and tried to jump over a herd of wandering cattle. It landed across the back of an African cow—which would have been funny except that the rider was seriously injured by his mishap.

Passing-out day, under the alert eye of Colonel Billy Bodle of Matabele Rebellion fame, was always a great, but nerve-racking occasion. It was called "Bashi Bazooks". I suppose we should have been reassured to see two or three ambulances bumping across the veldt to space themselves out around us as we took our places on the testing ground, but in fact those ambulances brought our hearts leaping into our mouths.

Four recruits at a time, starting at the 1,000-yards range, had to gallop in a semi-circle to the 100-yards range, dismount and fire five rounds of live ammunition. Next, they galloped back in a semi-circle to the 300-yards range, dismounted, fired five rounds—and so on, non-stop, from one butt to another. The fun of the exercise (for the onlooker) was that No. 3 had to remain mounted and hold the horses whilst the firing was going on, almost under their noses. Then, after the finish of the shooting, which had startled and excited the animals, the other men had to attempt to remount. It was not unknown for a recruit to get his foot caught in the nearside stirrup of the plunging horse alongside his own, and if this happened he was lucky to escape without being split in half.

The sections were passed or failed in this test as a team, and, if the team failed, all its four members were doomed to a further period of training—which no one could think of with equanimity. After the rigours of the recruits' course, the un-certain joys of being posted to an outstation were eagerly an-ticipated.

I passed my recruit course from Salisbury, and was posted as troop clerk to Bulawayo at the end of 1908, under Captain St. John, a stern disciplinarian.

In Bulawayo I went to a boxing match, and saw a man named Jim Chapman deal out a severe hiding to an unpleasant bully of a Dutchman. After the fight I discovered that Chapman was an Australian—without money. He had been paid two pounds for the fight, and this sum was already spent in debt repayments. I gave him a shakedown at my own quarters. In return, Jim Chapman gave me boxing lessons. Some weeks later, when Christmas Day came, we had a party which the officers attended. A boxing ring was set up, and it was suggested that Chapman and I should give a sparring match.

We did our best, but nothing we could do, with gloves on, came anywhere near to the kind of violent fights that were not infrequent in and outside the canteen of a night. After our bout, a trooper called Watkins climbed up on to his long legs and asserted that he could knock the block off either of us, and particularly Sillitoe.

"Go on, Sillitoe," said one of the officers firmly. "You must do, man—never hold up your head again if you don't!"

I knew he was right, although this wasn't turning out to be the sort of Christmas gaiety that I would have chosen for myself. Watkins stripped off his shirt and pulled gloves contemptuously on to his hairy fists, and I began to see that his conception of boxing was a broad-minded one. I soon realized that it was he or I for the count.

In the end I succeeded in knocking him out, and to bring him round his head was dipped into a bucket of water which turned horribly pink. My honour was saved and I felt at liberty to return to my quarters. When I was alone, I sat down rather unhappily on my bed. I was only twenty and the whole business had upset me very much—my first Christmas away from home, and I had celebrated the season of goodwill with a fight!

My next posting was to Nyamandhlovu, which means "Meat of the Elephant", in the Gwaai River country, and here my first job was to round up and arrest a Dutchman who was known to be somewhere out in the veldt, shooting game without a licence and making biltong (preserved meat) for black-market trade with the natives. This Dutchman was known as a good shot and an anti-social citizen. He knew I was on his trail, just as I knew in which directions he headed, for the bush and the veldt are both great whispering galleries, where every native could seem to cock his ear into the wind and tell you news accurately from a hundred miles distant. This man-hunt was an adventure such as I had always dreamed of, and I considered it an ample reward for the tedious hardships of my training.

When I caught up with my man I found him to be a tall, loose-limbed, dirty, bearded Boer, who glowered resentfully and surrendered his rifle with very considerable reluctance. How he had been using it was obvious from the strips of meat strung over sticks and drying in the sun and by small, smoking, wood fires. I had the impression that he did not at all appreciate being taken into custody by a lad just out of his 'teens.

However, I, in my pride at capturing him, felt no personal animosity whatsoever. Magnanimously I explained to him that, provided he would give me his word of honour to make no trouble, I would dispense with the use of handcuffs—they would be a nuisance to both of us and uncomfortable for him. He answered sullenly: "I will come upon my honour." Gratified, I returned the handcuffs to my saddle-bag.

That night he escaped, taking my horse with him.

The first of the B.S.A. precepts—on the subject of drunkenness—had never worried me as at that time I did not drink at all. The second precept was: "Never come back without your man," and at that moment it was worrying me a great deal. I commented to myself on my predicament in a few brief telling phrases and set out again in pursuit. The position was simple. He had my horse and I had my feet. Therefore, in order not to be left behind I must put in extra time travelling. This meant that I had to keep going while he slept. It took me about four days to catch up with him again and by that time I was not in a pleasant mood, particularly when I found he had misused my horse until it had gone lame.

From then onwards, I kept him handcuffed to my stirrup-leather until we reached the nearest point of the railway line that ran on single track from the Congo border south to Nyamandhlovu, a further sixty miles away. I was young, and better able to manage without sleep than my captive, and I kept him going at a lively pace. When the train came, fourteen hours late, it was "limping", for it had ploughed through a herd of elephant and had knocked several of them over. In their agonies and indignations, the fallen animals had kicked at the train as it passed, and smashed great gaping holes in the sides of many of the trucks. The cowcatcher of the engine had been completely ripped away. The iron steps of the engine itself, and those of all the coaches, had been kicked into fantastic shapes, and four of the coaches were so smashed that they could not continue. But the rest of the train came on, and it was a good enough conveyance to reach Nyamandhlovu without further incident. I must admit that the Dutchman was in a rather sorry state of exhaustion by the time we arrived at my outstation—but I can't say I cared.

It is surprising how much of a policeman's success in his career depends upon his being able to keep awake—and this is as true in England as I found it to be on the African veldt. Once, my failure to keep awake when it was my duty to do so was responsible for a man coming near to losing his life. I had been given the task of escorting a white man suffering from delirium tremens to the mental hospital at Bulawayo. I had to collect him at Livingstone, and the journey back by train took nineteen hours.

He had committed no crime except to lose his reason as a result of drink, a misfortune which was not by any means uncommon in Southern Rhodesia in those days. I did not feel it reasonable to handcuff him. Instead I decided to lock the railway compartment door and try to keep awake during the journey.

He lay down and pulled his blanket over his head. For the first hour or two he played a macabre game of pulling it down, peering at me with a sly chuckle, then pulling it up again over his face. Finally he went to sleep. The hours passed. The train was stuffy, the heat of the day grew, the wheels went churning monotonously on, and the sun-hazy vivid green landscape kept slipping by. . . . During the night I dozed off

—and awoke just in time to see in the dim carriage light my lunatic's rear about to disappear through the window of the trundling train.

Somehow I managed to grab his belt and, though he had been almost completely out of the window and was threshing wildly in his madness, I succeeded in dragging him back. A large, demented man bent on self-destruction is not easily hoisted in through the low window of a moving train and by the time he was safely inside the carriage again I was gasping for breath and soaked with sweat. With a deplorable lack of gratitude he proceeded to attack me, and as I felt in no condition to argue I "persuaded" him to lie down and continue his sleep. For the rest of the journey I sat without taking my eyes from him, dabbing my skinned knuckles with a handkerchief and trying to compose myself. He was still "asleep" when I got him into the mental hospital at Bulawayo and the medical officer looked rather thoughtful as he examined a large bruise on his patient's jaw.

"How did that happen, Sillitoe?" he asked.

"He didn't tell me," I replied briefly.

The medical officer decided he wouldn't press the point, and relieved my conscience by informing me the patient was not badly hurt. And I further reassured myself by reflecting that if he had been able to make his own sane choice, he would surely have preferred to be knocked out than to die of a broken neck.

In May 1910 I was at Victoria Falls, and came near to being killed by a wounded lion. I had been instructed by the corporal in charge of Victoria Falls to go on inspection patrol to Matetsi, which was a small farming station on the railway line, about thirty miles south of the Falls, over the open veldt—it was an ordinary duty patrol to visit outlying farmers. I was mounted on a mule, which was better suited than a horse for the rough trek, and had two pack-donkeys, my own native servant, and a native policeman. My servant, Jim, carried my tin washbasin and the cooking pots in a clanking bundle on his head.

As we approached the lonely Matetsi railway station, where the railway line curved, I heard a rifle shot in the distance, and with youthful enthusiasm, thought it might be some Dutch big-game poacher. I moved towards the sound of the shot, down the railway line, and after about ten minutes a herd of trek-oxen came stampeding down the track towards us. I shouted and waved at them, and they gradually halted, just ahead of us, then fell in behind and followed my little caval-cade towards Matetsi, where the main building, apart from the few wood and corrugated iron shanties, was a water tank for replenishing the railway engines.

As we clattered around the bend of the railway line, just before reaching Matetsi station, I heard a shout, and saw a white man on a small hill, waving his hat frantically.

I waved back. I had been in Africa long enough to under-stand the wonderful joy that it can bring to a European on some lonely outstation to see another white man, and it would have been against all the courtesies to have passed on without a halt for a meal, smoke, and chat together.

He shouted again, and faintly across the distance, I heard him seeming to say: "Come round the railway line!"

I waved back that I understood, but pointed towards a short cut that I knew, through the thick grass that grew nearly eight feet tall, off the track and over a river ford. He seemed to become even more frantic at this, and waved, with, as I thought, wild enthusiasm.

What I did not know was that he was actually shouting: "Look out—wounded lion!"

About twenty yards behind me my native servant followed with his bundle of pots and utensils on his head, and behind him came the native policeman with the pack-donkeys. As we approached the stream, which was clear and shallow and about fifteen yards wide, I decided to give my mule a well-deserved drink.

I had one foot out of the stirrup, and was actually swinging from the saddle, when there came a terrific, booming roar from the thick bushes just alongside me. A great, tawny lion was in the act of leaping at me, and as I saw him he passed right over the saddle on which, less than a second before, I had been sitting. The frightened mule bounded forward and, clutching desperately at it, I was dragged right across the river before being sent flying by a kick on the thigh from the poor beast who, at that moment, wanted most earnestly to be rid of my extra weight.

The lion splashed across the stream and paused about ten paces from me, snarling. It held up one of its front paws like a kitten about to pat a ball—but any resemblance to a playful gesture ended there. Its tail was making ominous flicks of rage.

My rifle had been jerked out of my hand and was also about ten paces from me—the lion, the rifle, and myself forming a triangle. I became abruptly aware that I might well be killed. My only hope was to get the rifle before the lion could get me, and at such a moment one realizes poignantly that in agility the average human is not much of a match for a lion.

Just then, my native servant, who had heard the roar, stole cautiously into view through the long grass. He saw me—and then he saw the lion! With a yell of terror, he flung down his bundle and dived headlong into a pool in the stream, under whose waters he managed to remain for an incredibly long time.

The yell, splash, and clatter as tin bowl, cooking pots, and dishes burst from their wrappings and went bouncing in all directions upset the lion. This was a development he had not foreseen. Shrewdly he decided to retire into the bush to take thought.

This respite enabled me to reach my rifle, and, though I was badly shaken, and injured by the mule's kick, with my rifle in my hands I felt the danger had diminished to manageable proportions.

Presently the European who had waved a warning at me came down a narrow native path through the tall grass, and I went with him to his camp. It was he who had fired the shot I heard as I approached Matetsi. He had outspanned his oxen to graze, heard the lion roar and saw him leap on the back of one fear-crazed black ox, grab its muzzle with his paw as the beast galloped, and pull back its head until the neck snapped. Then he had ripped out the ox's throat and was lapping the blood. My new friend had then taken the shot I had heard—but by only wounding the lion, had made it even more dangerous.

My friend, whose name turned out to be Cummings, dressed my injured thigh, and assured me no bones were broken. I also ascertained that my hair had not turned white, and was relieved but incredulous.

That same afternoon Cummings and I went out to hunt the lion. We found seven lions altogether and managed to shoot two each, but the dense bush and long grass made it too dangerous for us to look for them afterwards. Luckily, however, one of my lions dropped where I could see him, and I took his skin back with me to Victoria Falls, convinced, by the fact that he had two bullet wounds, that he was the one who had attacked me.

My next posting was back to Bulawayo in July 1910, and I found that the disciplinarian Captain St. John had been replaced there by Captain Murray, whom I was soon to credit with great perspicacity since he decided I deserved promotion. On 12th October of that year he made me a corporal, and, when the Regimental Sergeant-Major pinned the stripes on my arm, I felt that I was experiencing the greatest moment of my life. I think it may have been that indeed, for I know of nothing that I have since achieved that has given me such unadulterated satisfaction as this promotion.

I was now given the privilege of choosing my new duty station, and without hesitation I chose Victoria Falls, which, although not over-healthy (I suffered my first dose of malaria fever there) had an unsurpassed magnificence which compensated for any disadvantages. As Corporal in charge it was my duty, and my pleasure also, to explore the Falls from every approachable aspect, in order to know the terrain of my station. Visitors arrived from all parts of the world, and, naturally, there was no better guide to the famous Falls than the blue-and-khaki-uniformed Corporal of the British South Africa Police. I must say I grew as proud of the Falls as if I had contrived them myself and was most eager that they should be admired. On one occasion I took an American family around, showing them the view from the western end by the Devil's Cataract where the Livingstone Monument now stands. The Victoria Falls extend for one and a quarter miles with a 400-foot drop, and this is an unfailing source of amazement to American visitors who are always flabbergasted to discover that they are bigger than their own more publicized Niagara Falls. This particular American stood there and stared in real dismay over the stupendous cataract. Then he turned to me and said brokenly: "I guess Niagara is just perspiration!" I was delighted.

In my capacity as guide, I enjoyed one great privilege. My life in Africa did not afford me outstandingly good opportunities for finding feminine company, but at Victoria Falls at least, I had an advantage—for any girl who stayed at the Victoria Falls Hotel was determined to see the lunar rainbow from the bridge that spans the gorge of the Zambesi, and who but I was qualified to show her this most romantic and wonderful phenomenon of the African night?

My stay at Victoria Falls lasted less time than I had anticipated, for not long after my arrival I received word from Colonel Sinclair that his father-in-law, Sir John Jackson, was intending to visit the Falls and would look me up. When Sir John arrived, he asked me most kindly if there was any way in which he could be of service to me and I mentioned my ambition to win a commission with the police in the Northern Rhodesia territory which, like Southern Rhodesia, was administered under Royal Charter by the British South Africa Company.

Sir John was apparently satisfied with what he learned of me, for he recommended me to the Board of Directors of the Company. In February of the following year I crossed the Zambesi River for an interview in Livingstone, and almost immediately I was granted my commission. The one pip on each shoulder of a second-lieutenant did not arouse in me quite the same rapturous pride as had my Corporal's stripes, but I knew that this commission was an important rung of the ladder I had set out to climb.

CHAPTER THREE

Life at Livingstone – Elephant hunting – I return to England on sick leave, and become engaged – My police post at Lusaka.

THE Northern Rhodesia Police, like their colleagues in Southern Rhodesia, were the first line of defence in case of war, serving not only to maintain law and order but also as the cadre of an emergency army. In Northern Rhodesia the only Europeans in the force were the officers and a few N.C.O.s, the rank and file being all natives, drawn mostly from the north-east of the country and from Nyasaland. They were known as "Askaris", the native name for soldiers, and, indeed, when war did come they proved to be very fine ones.

However, that was in an unimaginable future, and meantime life at Livingstone was very agreeable for a twenty-two-year-old lieutenant. There were sundown parties and dinners, plenty of sport, and the comforts of a well-appointed mess.

Often we used to make up a party to cross the Zambesi and call in at the Victoria Falls Hotel for drinks. This meant driving three or four miles in a Cape-cart drawn by mules from our Police Headquarters to the north side of the river. Then we travelled downstream in a canoe to the landing stage on the south bank which was not more than about a mile from the hotel. We always chose one of the two or three nights a week when a train ran to Livingstone from the south, so that we could make our return journey after dark by rail.

One memorable night, however, the train did not turn up. To be perfectly fair, it is possible that we missed it. At all events, we stood waiting vainly for a long time by the deserted railway track, and eventually it dawned on us that we should have to get back to Livingstone by some other means. If we did not report for early morning parade next day no explanations or excuses were likely to prevent serious measures being taken to punish us and I began to see my whole career jeopardized.

We could scarcely walk back along the railway line. Our thin shoes would never have stood up to at least seven miles of very rough going and it would be no good at all to arrive for parade incapacitated by injured feet. So we decided to take a canoe and paddle upstream across the river and back to the north-side landing stage. We did not regard the decision as a particularly rash one—after all, there were four of us, all young and vigorous—and on the face of it there was nothing very hazardous in paddling the canoe upstream even in darkness.

But we were certainly very lucky to manage it. We paddled at random, dodging rocks purely by the grace of God. The swiftly-running current kept breaking into fierce little rapids, every now and again a hippo would bob up out of the water, disconcertingly close. We could not paddle near shore because of the dangerous jutting rocks and tangled undergrowth, and all the time we were unhappily aware that less than a mile away was a thundering, 400-foot cascade of water rushing into the gorge below. If the canoe had overturned we should have had no chance at all of making the bank.

By the time we reached Headquarters, it was early daylight —and no more subdued party of merrymakers ever came home with the milk.

Towards the end of my first year with the N.R.P. I was sent as escort officer to the Anglo-Belge Boundary Commission, which had the task of demarcating the boundary between Northern Rhodesia and the Belgian Congo. My own job was to protect the party, and to use my knowledge of the country and its problems to keep it as safe as possible from the unwelcome attentions of local tribes who might prove hostile.

It was during this job that I shot my first elephant. I had naturally been eager to accomplish this classic feat as soon as possible since such wonderful opportunities presented themselves in this almost virgin country. Elephant hunting is, I suppose, a most dangerous sport, for although very short-sighted the elephant has an extraordinarily keen sense of smell, and once he has scented you he becomes a most formidable foe. The first advice I received from experienced hunters was to hang from the barrel of my rifle a piece of cotton which, when one is standing still, indicates immediately any change—however slight—in the direction of the wind which might betray one's presence to the quarry.

The usual routine of a herd of elephants is that, as soon as they start to move, at daybreak or soon after, the cows and calves go off to feed, often protected by a male sentry—a tuskless bull, called a "tonde", who protects the cows from any enemies in return for assistance in feeding. (The unfortunate tonde, having no tusks, would not be able without this help to split the tree bark which elephants like to chew.) The first thing to do, therefore, after ascertaining where elephant are to be found, is to measure the size of the footprints in order to follow the larger tracks of the bulls while allowing the cows and tonde to go their way.

I set out with a little native hunter called Kumbyamtela who was to prove invaluable. After following the tracks for many miles we were eventually able to sort the bulls from the cows—without, of course, being able to see them in the dense forest. Keeping a careful watch for a change in the wind, we crept up on our prey, tense with excitement as we heard an occasional trumpeting or the crash of a tree. It is supremely important to get as close as possible to your elephant—not more than thirty to fifty yards distant—so that you can be reasonably certain of hitting a vital spot. At last the moment arrived when, simultaneously, Kumbyamtela and I saw about twenty yards away a huge grey mass. The elephant was broadside on, so we had obviously approached without arousing his suspicions. I crept ahead and aimed with my Martini-Enfield single-loading rifle at the brain, between the eye and ear. I could not afford a sporting rifle with its superior power and so I knew that I must rely on accuracy of aim.

My shot was a fatal one and the elephant never moved, but collapsed heavily where he stood. Immediately pandemonium broke loose. I was, frankly, quite unprepared for the appalling noise made by a whole herd of elephants stampeding in all directions, knocking down trees and trumpeting madly in their terror.

Almost immediately another elephant ran between me and the one I had shot. I was fortunate enough to drop him, too, with a single shot. Then as I stood behind a large tree, I saw bearing down on me from the far side of the first elephant an enraged tonde, his huge ears flapping and a very strong sense of purpose about him. With my small-bore rifle (a .303) I had, of course, no chance of stopping him with a frontal shot. I could only hope to prevent him getting my wind. I beckoned to Kumbyamtela and rapidly we crawled as low to the ground as possible until we lay behind the second dead elephant. Here we were safe, for his smell was greater than ours, and shielded us. We remained there an interminable time, peeping occasionally to spy on our enemy, the tonde. Eventually, not having found us, he decided, no doubt, that it was his duty to go off in search of the stampeded cows. We watched with a huge sigh of relief as he disappeared into the dense forest.

The news of our kill soon spread to villages round about and natives came from miles away to gorge themselves on the meat which they consider a great delicacy. The tusks were removed and the fatty interiors extracted—which took a considerable time—and then there was a ceremony to propitiate the spirits and show our gratitude for their protection.

For me, the greatest delight was still to come. For when I got back to camp I found that the tusks of my two elephants weighed, together, over 200 lb. I sold the ivory at ten shillings a pound and, since my licence had cost me no more than £25, I considered my little expedition a highly remunerative one. Admittedly, other hunters have enjoyed even greater good fortune, bringing back tusks weighing over 100 lb. each. But as a beginner I felt I had no reason to be ashamed of my achievement.

The great numbers of game of every description in this previously unexplored heart of the bush were exceeded only by the millions of malaria-infected mosquitoes. I was frequently urged by the medical officer who was with us to take quinine regularly and use a mosquito net always at night, but a young man tends to treat such dangers casually, and I neglected these wise precautions. The not surprising result was that I began to suffer frequent bouts of malaria, and when I returned to Livingstone at the end of 1912, after having been with the Boundary Commission for nearly a year, I discovered I had contracted blackwater fever. It was a very unpleasant shock. Even in Livingstone, with a European hospital, men frequently died from blackwater fever, and if I had contracted it at any time during my months in the bush, it would without doubt have proved fatal. But I was lucky.

As a result of this misfortune, I went to England on sick leave early in 1913, and did not return until June of that year. I think I must be one of the very few men who have reason to remember blackwater fever with gratitude, but it was in fact as an indirect consequence of my illness that I happened to meet the person who has done more than any other to help and cheer me throughout my life. For on that return voyage on the *Gloucester Castle* I met the girl who was to become my wife.

I shall never forget walking up the gangway to the ship at Southampton, and staring—very rudely, no doubt—at a dark-haired young girl, sitting with her parents and a younger brother, on a seat facing me. If there is such a thing as love at first sight, this was most certainly it. Outraging all the conventions, I continued to stare, and it must have seemed to her father, a forthright Yorkshire businessman, that the lanky, fair young man was presuming a great deal when, a few minutes later—armed rather foolishly with a quoit ring—he smiled as ingratiatingly as he knew how and asked of the young lady if she played quoits.

Dollie Watson seemed as keen on the game of quoits as I did, and from that beginning on the *Gloucester Castle* we started our romance. She was the daughter of Mr. and Mrs. John Watson of Hull, and they, with their son Cecil, were making the voyage out to Durban to visit their elder son Bernard who was sugar planting. The *Gloucester Castle* took twenty-one days to reach the Cape, and by the end of the voyage Dollie and I were engaged. Her father made no objection, but he brought her on a visit to Livingstone to see me on my "home ground". It seems that he was quite satisfied with the impressions he gained there.

We parted light-heartedly enough, full of plans for an early reunion. Alas! it was seven years before we met again, and between our meetings the world went mad. Somehow, though, with no more to remember than a few weeks on board ship, we both remained sure of our love, and four months after our eventual reunion we were married—as we had never doubted we should be.

Meantime, however, I was busy. Immediately after Dollie left to return to England, I was sent from Livingstone to open a police post at Lusaka, to-day the capital of Northern Rhodesia but in those days little more than a cluster of huts round a tiny hotel and a blacksmith's shop for the repair of trek wagons, with, some distance away, a lime kiln worked by a Greek named Marapodi. The well which I helped to sink so that we could have a reliable water supply is still used to-day; those few huts have evolved into a flourishing town, the most important rail stop on the line running north into the Belgian Congo.

My main task was the prevention of big-game poaching by Dutchmen, who were much addicted to this habit. Many of them were crack shots and did a fine trade making biltong of their kill and bartering it among the native tribes for mealie meal.

I had taken with me two European sergeants, both of whom had served previously in the Metropolitan Police. However, as they had little experience of the country, they usually stayed in the camp while I did the patrolling. My most entertaining companion was Charlie Warriner, employed by the Public Works Department. He was general handy man and could, given a few tools, tackle any practical problem and build anything. This was useful, as, apart from sinking the well, we had also to erect living quarters consisting of pole-and-daaga thatched huts. Charlie was the only person there who had the slightest idea of the technicalities involved in these jobs, especially when, in making the well, we were blasting through hard limestone—a ticklish enough task even for a fully-fledged engineer.

In these circumstances I think it was understandable that when the Acting Administrator, Mr. McKinnon, did us the honour of inspecting our outpost, we were confidently expecting that he would murmur a word or two of praise. But, accompanied by a haughty A.D.C., he viewed the well, and then, with the great dignity which is not uncommon to administrators and governors of colonies, he remarked: "I don't think, Warriner, that you are sinking this well quickly enough."

In Africa speech is free, but, as a well-disciplined officer, standing rigid in the presence of a high Administrator, I was not expecting Charlie's tart reply: "If you don't think I'm doing it quick enough, Mister, then you'd better bloody well do it yourself!"

The A.D.C. achieved the expression of scandalized shock of a Bateman drawing, and the Administrator did not trust himself to speak another word. He stalked off, and the next development was a message from Livingstone that Warriner was to be dismissed for insubordination. However, as I could certainly never sink the well at all without Charlie's help, I managed to appeal successfully against this decision.

For my living quarters, I had two huts, each about twenty feet in diameter and with thirty feet between them. I used one as a living-room, the other as a bedroom.

Now, in Africa one quickly learns to accept the fact of man-killing lightning and I had a healthy respect for it because I had seen it. It is a fork-lightning, and every year in Africa it kills both men and cattle. If you are riding a sweaty horse through a storm, the only sensible thing to do—as every B.S.A. policeman knew—is to hobble the horse to a low bush and then lie flat on the ground about thirty yards away. It is exceedingly imprudent to remain the tallest object on the open veldt with a fork-lightning storm heading in your direction at a speed of fifty miles an hour.

Some Europeans in Africa spread wire-netting over their huts to act as a conductor, but at Lusaka we possessed no such refinements. However, I had not worried unduly until one day a dry storm began to brew. I had a guest for tea—the Assistant Magistrate from Chilanga—and, after washing in my bedroom hut, we were just sitting down in the "living-room" next door when there was a blinding flash with a peal of terrific thunder. The shock sent me spinning backwards over my chair, and by the time I had scrambled to my feet and run outside, my sleeping hut was ablaze.

With my servants, I rushed to rescue my possessions. The inside of the hut was an astonishing sight. The metal locks had been wrenched from my suitcases and the mirror had split into tiny fragments that were scattered everywhere. The most disastrous loss of all was my newly-acquired sporting rifle, its barrel now twisted and molten like wax that had been thrust into a furnace. On the floor was a peculiar sticky substance, but what it was I never discovered. My most feasible guess was that the quicksilvering of the mirror had undergone some chemical change: or else that this curious effect had been produced by tremendous heat on the hard-packed floor of earth and cattle dung.

The Assistant Magistrate and I escaped with a slight shock-burn each and we had not had time even to feel afraid. But it was sobering to reflect afterwards that we had been in the bedroom hut not more than one minute before it was struck.

We did not have any visitors at Lusaka, so we were all the more gratified to greet Sir Leander Starr Jameson ("Doctor Jim" of the Jameson Raid). He was, at the time of his visit to us, Prime Minister at the Cape, and had come in his capacity as a Director of the Chartered B.S.A. Company to talk with farmers. He stayed with us for two or three days and, to my great joy, authorized two mounted troopers from the B.S.A. Force in Southern Rhodesia to come and help me. Until then, my difficulties in patrolling adequately such a vast area had been immense.

On New Year's Eve, 1914, a most amazing sight was seen at Lusaka. An Argyll motor-car (Argylls still run, I believe, in the London-Brighton Veterans Rally) and a Triumph motor-cycle stormed into our little town. This was the "Cape to Cairo Motor Expedition", sponsored by the *Daily Telegraph*, and led by Captain R. N. Kelsey, with Mr. Pickersgill Cunliffe riding the motor-cycle, and a reporter and a co-driver completing the team.

In the arrival of this travel-stained and intrepid party, we found a splendid excuse for a celebration, and I remember how, with great solemnity, we all drank the King's health at the beginning of the New Year. It was as well for our good spirits that we had no premonition of the disastrous end to the expedition—Kelsey was killed by a leopard at Serenje shortly after he left Lusaka—nor of the world catastrophe which 1914 was holding in store for us all.

CHAPTER FOUR

Five hundred miles across country with a "museum piece" – My duties as an Assistant Political Officer – An enemy raid – My leopard-companion, Little Willie.

D<small>URING</small> the first weeks of the war the British forces were in difficulties on the Northern Rhodesia border. The Germans had a modern gunboat, the *Von Götzen*, on Tanganyika, and she swiftly captured two or three Belgian vessels and converted them into gunboats. This made a very serious situation indeed, and it remained so until, many months later, Commander Spicer-Simpson took charge of an expedition and brought two little gunboats from England virtually in sections, assembling them on the lake shores.

For some reason that was never clear to me, Spicer-Simpson named his midget "warships" *Mimi* and *Toutou*. Despite these frivolous names, however, they cleared the Lake of the German ships in a series of valiant actions, and so harassed *Von Götzen* that the Germans ultimately scuttled her at Kigoma to avoid her capture or destruction. She lay for years on the bottom of Tanganyika but, when eventually she was recovered, it was remarkable that, due to some chemical quality of the lake water, there were no signs of rust or deterioration. She was refloated in 1924 and still sails on the Lake as a passenger and freight vessel, under the name *Liemba*, flying the British flag.

However, in that hot, uncertain August of 1914, while England herself was bewilderingly unprepared for war, there was not a piece of British artillery larger than a machine gun in the whole of Northern Rhodesia.

Then somebody remembered a museum piece, an ancient muzzle-loading seven-pounder screw-gun, resting on its well-earned laurels in Southern Rhodesia. Hasty investigation showed that this weapon was still capable of being fired, and, as such, was better than nothing. From squatting muzzle-up on a parade-ground in Southern Rhodesia, with a plaque describing its former glories, this screw-gun became overnight the total artillery equipment of both Northern and Southern Rhodesia.

I received at Lusaka a top-priority telegraph message from our Colonel to go at once to Broken Hill, and wait for the gun to arrive there by train. Beforehand, I was to arrange with the District Commissioner for carriers and provisions. And then, post-haste, I was to take it to Abercorn on the edge of Lake Tanganyika. This would be a journey of 520 miles over nothing more progressive in the way of roads than the typical African single-file track or path from village to village. My orders impressed upon me that the gun must be taken to Abercorn at all speed, but gave no details about the weight of it. I could not, however, imagine that any piece of artillery could be successfully wheeled over such country through forests and across rivers. It became apparent to me that we should have to carry our gun for most of the journey.

The District Commissioner at Broken Hill, infected by the general excitement, made rapid arrangements for me to have as many native porters as I needed. I chose six hundred, prepared food and safari packs for the party, and then settled down to wait for the gun to arrive.

It came, fortunately accompanied by Corporal Jack Horton and three European B.S.A. Police troopers who were trained gunners. With them came two hundred rounds of black powder ammunition. The gun itself was smothered in brown grease that dripped in the hot sunshine. It was only a tiny gun judged by comparison with modern artillery, but even to-day I think it would look huge to anyone who knew that he was to be responsible for carrying it 520 miles. I approached it with nearly as much awe as my native bearers felt, who were so impressed that they began immediately to compose a song about our proposed pilgrimage.

When we had dismantled the gun I discovered that the heaviest piece—the barrel—weighed fully two hundred pounds. A cradle had to be made for it so that four porters could share the burden on their shoulders.

Then we set off, pushing and pulling with ropes wherever the ground would allow it, and looking like a parody of a triumphal procession. When the going became too tough we unscrewed everything that would twist and carried the dismembered bits as pack-loads. Altogether the weight was over a thousand pounds, and, apart from the gun itself and our own provisions, the two hundred rounds of ammunition alone required a hundred porters. However, we conveyed that gun to Abercorn at an average speed of eighteen miles each day, and arrived after thirty days.

By this time the Germans had landed at Kasakalawe in Northern Rhodesia territory at the south-east corner of Tanganyika. I was, therefore, instructed to join a composite body of British and Belgian troops under Colonel Stennett and take the gun to a spot suitable for attacking the *Von Götzen*. However, I was sent ahead with my company to reconnoitre first without the gun, and we found ourselves unexpectedly obliged to engage the *Von Götzen*, relying on machine-gun fire only. So I received my baptism of fire, but, before our gun could be brought to the scene of action, the Germans had departed.

Back at Abercorn, I continued to wait hopefully to see it in action, but was eventually ordered south again before it had gone into the firing line. Eventually it was moved to Saisi, a few miles east of Abercorn, and there it helped to repel an attack by the Germans—who had themselves managed to unearth a couple of very similar museum pieces. I must say, I was disappointed not to be present to witness my gun's success. I was told that Farrow, one of our four gunners, who was something of a wag, insisted on signalling "outers" and "inners" at each shot the Germans fired during the prehistoric artillery duel. But I fear that this sporting attitude to the war faded soon afterwards.

Now a captain, I passed the next couple of years fighting with my company of Askaris over an enormous area of country. Then, in 1916, I went down with enteric fever, after which I was sent to Johannesburg to recuperate.

During these first two years of war a very large part of German East Africa had been conquered by the troops of General Smuts who had come in from the north, and by General Northey's army from Northern Rhodesia and Nyasaland. When I returned from Johannesburg I was sent to Zomba, the capital of Nyasaland, where General Northey had his headquarters. At this time the captured German territory was being taken over by British occupying forces, and I was informed that Northey had selected me to become an Assistant Political Officer in the conquered territory. I fancy this was because someone had noted I was described as having an extensive knowledge of Chinyanja, the official native language, and also some Chiwemba. This was promotion—if a staff job can be so considered by an infantry officer—but it meant losing the comradeship of my Company which had been a great comfort to me while we were fighting. However, I had no alternative but to report to the Bismarkburg Province in the south-west corner of German East Africa, adjoining Lake Tanganyika, and take up my new duties, though, knowing my regiment to be involved in heavy fighting in other parts of German East Africa, I felt acute distress at abandoning it. I could not help but feel that I was going to a comparatively soft job while others were bearing the brunt of the danger—though in the end the soft job proved to be one of the most dangerous I ever had.

From the Bismarkburg Province I was posted to take over the sub-district of Ilunde, about 250 miles away and 150 miles south of Tabora on the central railway line that runs between Dar-es-Salaam and Kigoma on Lake Tanganyika.

My task was to establish British prestige among the native tribes of the district, many of whom had seldom, if ever before, seen a white man. To add power to prestige, I had been allotted a retinue of six untrained natives, euphemistically described as policemen. They were not even accredited Askaris. They had rifles and vague notions of how to use them, but they had not the remotest conception of what the duties of a native policeman might be. Still, they were a stout-hearted bunch and perfectly content to give me their unquestioning loyalty.

The district swarmed with tsetse fly, but this was a normal worry in Central Africa. I was more concerned to realize that Ilunde swarmed also with marauding bands of German Askari deserters, who, having seen active service with the Germans, were lavishly equipped with arms and ammunition stolen from their masters. They were now roaming across the territory in bands of various sizes and were very formidable raiders, having all the natural advantages of the native combined with the additional assets of European arms and military training.

However, with time on my hands, I soon had my six natives smartly drilled and well on the way to being excellent shots, and I was even able to begin teaching them police duties.

Then, one evening as the light was fading, I got word from natives in the district that a force of two Germans and twenty Askaris was coming to attack my little headquarters. It was no mere prowling band, but a determined and organized attempt to wipe out my station, and the force was reported to be less than a day's march away. This was most serious. I promptly sent each of my six policemen in different directions to fetch the native chiefs from every tribe within a few miles radius. Whilst the messengers were on their way I got the natives from the nearest village to build an enormous bonfire.

During that night a large crowd of natives collected. They came silently out of the darkness and assembled around the great fire, watchfully. They all knew the Germans were coming, for there is little that an African native on his own ground does not know. There were about three hundred of them, with others still drifting in.

By this time I could speak Swahili fluently, and I spoke to them by the firelight. I said: "The Germans are coming with men and guns." The eyes of my audience rolled as they listened in absolute silence. Then I went on: "The Germans know that you have been friendly to me. If they do not kill you they will certainly steal your food and burn your villages. Do you want me as a friend, or do you want the Germans to come back?"

They decided they preferred me. Put that way, the poor

devils hadn't much choice. So I had now a defence of three hundred men, who were armed with hunting spears and some comically ancient muskets dating from around 1800 which would not in any circumstances fire.

I told the chiefs to send out scouts to find where the Germans were, and in the few hours before daylight I set out with my supporters. I realized that if I was to hope to survive I would have to shoot both Germans myself, and, if possible, do this before they had managed to fire too many shots at my "army", which, being completely unused to facing bullets—or even to the noise of guns—could hardly be expected to stand up to almost a platoon of trained Askaris.

I was lucky, as usual. One of my scouts was captured by the Germans and, under a certain amount of pressure, told them that I was approaching at the head of an enormous crowd of armed natives to destroy them. This was true. He also told the Germans that my little army had "many guns", which was true only so far as a handful of museum pieces, including flint-locks without flints and muzzle-loaders without ramrods, ball, or powder, are describable as "many guns".

But it was enough for the Germans, who turned aside and disappeared into the bush. I never saw or heard of them again.

I stayed at this station for nine months and did not see another white man. I took a census and discovered there were 20,000 people in my territory—all natives, and so widely spread over the vast district that one could travel for days between villages. I used to awake in the mornings to find marks where lions had slept, pressed against the shelter of my hut. I had to stay inside my hut from nightfall until next day's daylight, for nothing could make going outside worth the risk of treading on an unfriendly member of the cat tribe in the darkness.

One morning my native servant found a young leopard in the hollow of a tree not very far distant from my hut. It was a friendly, soft and lovable little creature, very newly born, with paws gentle as a kitten. It mewed with hunger. I stuck a straw into a bottle-cork and let it suck diluted condensed milk. It was the best I could think to do, and my little foundling thrived.

I raised this young leopard cub. He would play with a ball like a dog, chase after it and fetch it back to my feet. At night he slept on my bed, purring throatily; and I began to find a sense of companionship in the noise. He seemed to look upon me as his mother, and I suppose there was some justification for this. After all, I had fed him!

I named him Little Willie, and he became a real companion to me. When I had to go shooting for the pot, I left Willie at home. When I was away he was always restless, and after a while would come and stalk me, low on his belly, then jump suddenly out of a bush and spring on to my shoulder, rubbing himself against my face and neck like a cat, throbbing with his own peculiar leopard's purr, a sort of snuffle.

Willie had no time for the natives. When he was about a year old he took to playing a game which consisted of hiding in a surface drain, jumping out on their backs as they passed and pulling off their loin cloths. He didn't hurt them really, but he was quite a hefty leopard by this time and they were rather scared of him.

One hot day, Willie got inside my office safe where it was cool. When I bent to pull him out, saying: "Come on, Willie—time for lunch!" he was asleep. Awaking suddenly, he put his teeth into my hand—I carry the scars to this day. I cuffed him and pulled him out, and he looked very contrite. There had been no malice in his bite (nor in my cuffing). It was just an accident between friends, when the "wild" had momentarily overcome his domestication.

When, after months of unbroken solitude, my relief officer came, I was seized with an uncontrollable desire to talk. I started, and continued, on and on and on. It was such a comfort to have another white man there and to have at last an opportunity to speak my own language that I chattered right through that day and far into the night. Captain Morgans, my relieving officer, listened to me sympathetically for as long as he could, but in the end I began to drive the poor chap frantic and he beseeched me with some vehemence to shut up.

It was good to be relieved from my duties at Ilunde, and from the inescapable solitude. But my pleasure had one considerable dark cloud. Captain Morgans did not wish to have anything to do with Willie. I tried to assure him that Willie was harmless, but it became apparent that Willie's harmlessness extended itself no further than me. He didn't want anything to do with Morgans. I tried then to persuade each of the native chiefs in turn to give shelter to him, but they were all too afraid and implored me to take him away. This was of course, impossible—a serving officer in wartime could scarcely lug a great leopard about with him from one duty station to the next. I did not know what to do.

"I'll shoot him for you," said Morgans, who realized my difficulty. He called the wretched Willie out of my hut, gave him a bone and shot him clean through the heart. It was a straight and merciful shot, and Willie leapt high in the air.

But although he was mortally wounded, he managed to crawl back into my hut and into my cramped little bedroom and when I went to find him he had laid himself at the foot of my bed and was dead. He had been my only companion for nine months, and I buried him sorrowfully, as some men would bury a faithful dog, with a stone to mark his grave in the bush.

Poor Morgans discovered that the solitary life at Ilunde was too much for him and after a few months he had to apply to be relieved. Later I learned that the man who was sent to take over from him had a nervous breakdown within three or four months, and after this the Ilunde station was closed down. It may be that the companionship of even a half-wild leopard made all the difference.

CHAPTER FIVE

Acting District Political Officer – The fight against famine – Return to Livingstone and resignation from the B.S.A.P. – My marriage, and return to Africa in the Colonial Service – Trouble with "King" Ntare and the Banyaruanda – I contract rheumatic fever and undergo a native cure.

IT was an enjoyable change for me to be posted to Tabora, which was situated in a comparatively civilized district in the middle of the central railway line that runs between Dar-es-Salaam and Kigoma. The town of Tabora was so important that the Standard Bank had actually opened a branch there, with two Europeans on the staff. Besides the large native population of Swahili and Arabs, there were also numerous European officers and N.C.O.s of the King's African Rifles, and a dozen or more European officials of the civilian administration, including police.

For me, life and work in Tabora were very pleasant. It was good to speak English again and to take a constructive part in helping to build up a British administration in that part of Africa. There was play, too—parties, tennis, shooting. I began to forget the solitude of Ilunde.

At the end of 1918 I was promoted to Acting District Political Officer, and posted to the important town of Dodoma, further westward along the railway line. I was made responsible for three sub-stations, in a district roughly the size of Yorkshire.

In such towns as Dodoma and Tabora, the Government headquarters is built in the shape of a sturdy stone fortress, known as the "Boma", and my quarters in the Boma at Dodoma were exceptionally comfortable.

I had no sooner taken over this appointment than a most appalling famine broke out over the entire province. The unfortunate natives were paying a tragic price for a war which had, in its origins, little enough to do with them. The Germans had requisitioned and looted their grain stores, cattle, and crops. Nor had the British been blameless. Following upon this, came two years of disastrous drought, when the arable land literally dried up and blew away. The natives were soon dying as thick and helpless as winter flies, and although we made frantic appeals for assistance to neighbouring provinces, there was so little grain and food to be found in the entire countryside that I had to send as far as South Africa before I could get supplies of the vital foodstuffs—mostly mealies— that were needed to stem the deathroll and check the spread of the many diseases that were springing up with nightmarish rapidity, as they always do in the wake of a tropical famine. We had to distribute mealies, and all the supplies had to be carried to our outlying districts. Native porters were almost as scarce as the foodstuffs—for natives simply hadn't the strength to carry loads; so every European in Dodoma gave a hand, working night and day. I myself drove a lorry many hundreds of miles over rough tracks during those hideous, heart-rending weeks.

In the middle of this desperate scramble against starvation and disease and death a balding, ginger-haired little man of middle age arrived at Dodoma. His name, he said, was Stones, and he was a Church Missionary Society doctor.

I shall never forget seeing his professional plate, nailed up alongside his native-built dwelling-hut. It read: "R. Y. Stones, M.D., F.R.C.S."

He was a wonderful man, full of courage that took him always far beyond his physical strength in works of mercy. He laid into that famine like the true man of God that he was, and dealt with dysentery, malnutrition, and the incidental saving of souls, with an infectious zeal that inspired us all.

He didn't say much. Somewhere, obviously, he had given up a first-class practice, to come to this place. Numerous times Dr. Stones performed intricate eye operations with the barest surgical equipment, and many a native around Dodoma district had him to thank for his preserved eyesight. I never knew his full story, but what I saw of these late chapters of it has made me certain that it must have been a very fine one.

I stayed a year at Dodoma, and when my duties there ended, I returned to Livingstone, making a never-to-be-forgotten trip which showed me all the splendours of Africa as I had imagined them to be while I was a child dreaming of such things, when the Volunteers brought their assegai and hide-shield trophies into St. Paul's Cathedral. I came down through Kigoma and across Lake Tanganyika to the Belgian Congo, then by stern-wheeler on the River Lualaba, down to the railway line at Elizabethville. This part of the journey took about a fortnight because of delays caused by sandbanks, and so on. We could travel only by daylight, and so were able to see the huge variety of game which is incredibly fascinating.

At Sakania, on the border of the Congo and Northern Rhodesia, I wrote out a telegram to be despatched to the Commandant of the Northern Rhodesia Police, Colonel Stennett, informing him that my duties as District Political Officer were ended, and that I was travelling back to report to him.

Unfortunately this telegram was never delivered. So when I reached Livingstone on New Year's Day, 1920, having been away since 1914, there was nobody to meet me at the station. Nobody expected me. And when I made my own way to Police Headquarters, I was greeted like a ghost from the past. Nor was I, it seemed, an entirely welcome ghost. It had not been explained to anybody why I had not returned to active service with my Askari company, and here I was, with the war comfortably ended, apparently turning up for my job back.

That was how it must have appeared to some of my brother officers. At any rate, nobody seemed to wish to be troubled to discover what had actually happened. My reception was aloof, almost to the point of coldness, and it was such a bitter blow to me, after my joyful anticipation on that prolonged journey, that I decided to resign my commission in the Police and to accept an appointment that had been offered to me in the Colonial Service.

Before I took up my appointment, however, I returned to

England, and was met at Waterloo Station by Dollie, my fiancée, who had not forgotten me. Four months later we were married, having found no difficulty in resuming our courtship from the point where war had intervened, seven years before. Our wedding took place in June, at the little village church of Elloughton, near Brough in East Yorkshire, and our honeymoon was brief—indeed, the latter part of it consisted of a journey back to Tanganyika for me to take up service under the Colonial Office.

After doing some temporary work at the capital, Dar-es-Salaam, I was posted back to Tabora. Here, life provided Dollie with novel interests. I don't think she ever became quite reconciled to our taking a loaded rifle with us when we accepted an invitation to dinner with our neighbours, nor to our walking between native servants with lanterns to scare away any lurking lions.

The first time Dollie heard a lion roar outside a zoo, it was one which was standing directly beneath her bedroom window —it took up its position outside our small wooden bungalow in the middle of the night and roared straight at her. She was not alone in being alarmed. We had been given in South Africa a beautiful Airedale terrier as a wedding present. We called him Peter and he was a magnificent chap and brave as the proverbial lion—except on this occasion when he came face-to-face with the real thing. When this lion roared outside our bedroom window, poor Peter's hair stood, quite literally, on end.

Towards the end of 1920, my wife found she was going to have a baby, and this was obviously not a suitable country for her in those circumstances. The medical services were very inadequate, and I was not prepared to take any risks. We made the sensible but saddening decision that Dollie should go home to England, to return when the baby was strong and well established.

It was a heartbreaking parting for us both, but the decision turned out to have been very wise. For, almost immediately after she had left, I was posted to the even more remote and wild outpost of Kasulo, in the heart of the Kigoma Province.

The Belgians had captured this district from the Germans with Ruanda and Urundi, and the typical German-built Boma at Kasulo looked like a fortress in the film version of *Beau Geste*. When the loot had been divided by the victors in 1921 it had been agreed that Kasulo should be given to the British, and my job was to go and take over from the Belgians.

I took six native police with me, and we performed with suitable solemnity the ceremony of lowering the Belgian flag and raising the Union Jack. The little Belgian Commissioner did not seem in the least reluctant to hand over Kasulo to the British. Before he left he invited me, as was proper, to meet the most powerful chief of the district. His was the warlike tribe of Banyaruanda, which came originally from the Ruanda Belgian Congo, and is one of the Batutsi tribes which originated in ancient Egypt. All these Batutsis are proud and difficult people. They are tall and statuesque and do not have the same facial structure as most African natives. Their king or queen is called "The Mwami", and there is another link with their ancient Egyptian origin in that the Mwami must always be of pure Ruanda blood and of the Royal lineage.

At the time I arrived in Kasulo, the elderly and respected king of the Banyaruandas had recently died, leaving the little "Prince" Kanyoni to succeed him. The regent was Senura, a peaceful man of learning.

Yet it was neither of these two whom the Belgian commissioner invited me to meet. I did not know the history of the Banyaruandas at the time, and was not aware that the king who was presented to me was in fact a usurper, a half-brother of little "Prince" Kanyoni, and not of pure Ruanda blood. His name was Nduyagwa.

Nevertheless, he called himself "King Ntare V", and when I saw him he looked very ugly, drunk, and insolent. He was surrounded by his courtiers and A.D.C.s, all armed and decorated, and grinning insolently.

Ntare made no attempt to rise or pay any other gesture of courtesy to me. Moreover, it looked to me, though I may have been wrong, that the Belgian Commissioner was a little afraid of him.

The Belgians, with a couple of platoons of well-drilled Askaris, marched out that same day, and left me and my six soldiers watching Ntare and his followers make off towards their respective villages.

Kasulo was a big district, about the size of Lancashire and Yorkshire together. There were other tribes in it, but Ntare was far and away the most powerful chief.

Very soon I began to get reports of villages being raided and burned down and cattle and women stolen. Ntare sent evasive answers to my messages, but it was obvious that he knew much more about it than he was prepared to discuss.

The raids and burnings continued. I began to make inquiries about "King" Ntare, and it was then that I discovered he was a usurper, and that the boy king was in hiding in the mission of the White Fathers at Mulera, forty miles away.

I sent for the boy and for Father Drost, the Father Superior of the Mission, to come and see me. The news of this must have flashed to Ntare, for within a few days I received word that a village less than ten miles from my Boma had been raided and mercilessly destroyed. Women had been raped and food stores looted.

This was an act of supreme insolence on the part of Ntare and was apparently his answer to my inquiries about himself. "King" Ntare wanted to play rough. I sent two policemen to his village with a message that the men who had attacked and pillaged the village were to be arrested and sent to me, and that Ntare was to accompany them. Back came his impudent answer that he had no intention of coming, that he was not going to arrest anybody, and that I was to mind my own business!

I sent another message, that if Chief Ntare did not come within two days, I would fetch him myself. For a while there was silence. Then a runner came panting in with news that Ntare was nearing my Boma with a large army of warriors.

An hour or two later I heard a great noise and shouting. With his warriors jigging around him, Ntare was advancing towards the Boma. He had about six hundred men and was leading the procession. There was a large flat assembly ground outside the stone walls of the Boma, and I instructed my native police that when he got there, they were to take out a chair and invite him to be seated. He was then to be told to assemble his men in a semi-circle, at fifty yards from the front of the Boma. I was not going to have a mob.

I posted three of my police at the entrance to the Boma's huge double doors. There was no other way in except over the sturdy walls.

I told my police I was going to have the guilty men flogged —for I had magisterial powers to give such punishment—and asked them to get a cane for me. A chair was carried out, and I sat down opposite Ntare. Once again he was slightly the worse for drink. He said: "You shall not give me orders, I am the king. I shall show these people that if they do not turn their thoughts in obedience to me and away from young Kanyoni, I will burn down their villages until they do obey me."

I said: "I want you to produce to me the leaders of those warriors of yours who burnt that village."

Contemptuously Ntare called out three names. Three tall warriors from the ranks of those nearest to him came towards us. I asked: "Did you men burn this village?" They answered that they had done it for the "king".

Then I spoke to the whole crowd. I explained that it was not the way of British justice to allow this sort of thing. The proud Banyaruanda must choose their ruler according to their own laws. If Ntare were a full-blooded Ruanda, then as the elder, he was rightful king. If Kanyoni was the only full-blooded Ruanda, then he was the rightful king, though yet a child.

But this, I said, was not what concerned me at the moment. The villages must not be burned, and warriors must not become thieves. It had to be stopped.

"As the magistrate of this district I am going to punish you three men as a warning that this sort of behaviour will not be tolerated. You will now receive six lashes each."

My policemen took the nearest man, and laid him firmly on the ground. One held his arms and another held his feet, while the third laid six smart strokes across his bare buttocks.

Chief Ntare was too amazed to know what to say. He sat there with my eye upon him while his three men were each given six of the best and sent back to their places. They did not make a sound during the punishment, but a prolonged murmuring sigh arose from the six hundred who watched.

When it was done, I said: "If there is more of this robbing and burning, Ntare, the punishment will be much more severe."

The atmosphere was very tense indeed. I could see that Ntare was about to give some kind of order to his followers, and he was angry enough for it to have been an unwise one. With sudden inspiration I said: "Before the Belgians left Kasulo, they told me that you men of the Banyaruanda refused to pay your hut and poll tax. Now I want every man who has not paid his tax to step forward."

There was an instant of silence, and then the most astonishing thing happened: every man turned and fled! Spears and perhaps even bullets they were prepared to risk. They would take a flogging in silence. But at the mention of paying their taxes, they showed that they were at heart not far removed from their European brothers-under-the-skin. They ran like hares!

It was a splendid opportunity for me to discredit the unwholesome King Ntare the Fifth. As he gazed, wide-eyed and woeful, after his retreating followers, I shouted as loudly as I could, so that some, at least, of his fleeing tribesmen would hear:

"You are the great chief—call your men back. Let them hear your voice, and watch them obey!"

But they were running like deer. He said nothing.

Soon there was nobody left except myself, my three policemen, Ntare, and a couple of his more elderly A.D.C.s. Then I had a straight talk with him. I said: "My friend, you are not going back to your village. You are coming inside the Boma with me. I have a lot to say to you."

I had him put in a cell. Yet I knew it would be only a matter of hours before his followers gathered their wits and returned to rescue him. The Boma was solid and we had rifles, but it did not seem the best way of building up British prestige to withstand a siege by native tribesmen for the sake of an arrested bogus chief. Ntare was riddled with an unpleasant disease, and not fit to walk very far, but I could not in any event keep him at the Boma for ever. I therefore decided to send him to Kigoma on a stretcher of poles and grass, and I got some friendly natives who had no reason to love him to act as bearers.

The ordinary native path to Kigoma lay through Ntare's own villages, and it was certain that if I sent him that way he would be rescued, and blood would probably be shed.

There was another bush track that headed south-east and veered towards the railway line by a most roundabout approach. I decided that if Ntare's men intended to rescue him, they would not attack the Boma after they had heard their chief was being taken to Kigoma, but would lie in ambush along the Kigoma path.

So I took a chance, and sent Ntare by the indirect route. My spies soon told me that my guess had been correct. Ntare's followers did lie in ambush along the Kigoma path, and they missed the party with the hapless Ntare by nearly twenty miles!

By runner I sent details of my charges against Ntare, and after a month he was tried at Kigoma by Mr. Justice Walker, a puisne judge from Dar-es-Salaam. Many of his followers made a pilgrimage to Kigoma to watch the trial, and saw him sentenced to a term of imprisonment and banishment from the territory.

This incident, therefore, closed in a manner which was fairly satisfactory from my point of view. There was, however, a postscript. A highly unprepossessing witch-doctor of the Banyaruanda who had been an enthusiastic supporter of Ntare, proceeded to put a curse upon me, prophesying that within three months I should be dead, or forced to leave the territory as a cripple. His villainous, experienced eye must have detected the first signs of rheumatic fever that were developing in me at this time. When I heard of this curse, I knew for sure that I was in for it, because the symptoms that had been troubling me, and which I had been trying to persuade myself were of nothing so serious as rheumatic fever, now had this unwelcome but undoubtedly expert diagnosis.

Friendly witch-doctors came with their potions to visit me. I was soon in desperate pain, with my knee swollen until it was fully as big as my head. Father Drost heard of my plight through the native bush telegraph and walked forty miles through the bush to give me his precious supply of aspirin to ease my pain. This pain was so intense that once I intended to shoot myself, but when I managed to reach my revolver holster, I discovered that my good native servant Lawe had hidden my gun. I raved and threatened, but he bravely would not tell me where he had concealed it, for he guessed my intention. Father Drost, who was something of a herbalist, made poultices of celery and stewed strawberry leaves for me. He was a most wonderful nurse, and undoubtedly saved my life. All the same, there did come a time when I seemed to be about to die. My Airedale dog, Peter, who was usually faithful and affectionate, would not come into my room that day, but sprawled moaning at the door.

I had earlier offered a reward of £5 to any native who could relieve my pain, and I think it was probably only just in time that a very old and wrinkled witch-doctor came to try to earn this reward. He made a deep incision, shaped like a cross, in my fantastically swollen knee, and cupped it with a heated cows' horn. It was agonizingly painful, but nothing could have been much worse than the pain I was already in. After a few days of this treatment, the swelling was reduced, and I was glad to pay him his £5.

It was during my illness that a cable arrived by runner, telling me of the birth of our daughter, Audrey, in March 1921. I was so weak and exhausted that it was many days before I could write a cable to Dollie, who was anxiously waiting.

I was scarcely fit to travel when I was moved from Kasulo to Tanga on the coast. I was pale, ghostlike, and still very ill.

However, I was fortunate enough to discover traces of a natural hot sulphur spring that the Germans had found at Tanga. It was derelict and overgrown, but with the help of some native labour I got it cleaned up, and used to lie for hours

With the trophies from my first two elephants, shot while escort officer to the Anglo-Belge Boundary Commission in 1911

Dollie and I at Victoria Falls, 1913

A lieutenant in the N.R.P., with the Mkushi detachment in 1913

At Tabora, 1918

in it. At first I was stiff and crippled, but after each immersion
I became a little better. When I was much better I was transferred to Moshi at the base of Mount Kilimanjaro.

In 1922 I returned to Tanga. It was in this year that Dollie,
who had been distressed by news of my illness, came out to be
with me, leaving the baby in England in the care of her mother.
When she saw me, she was even more upset. I was as thin as a
rake, and although by this time I had achieved the rank of first
grade administrative officer, I decided I ought to leave Africa
with what health I had left. But could I find another job? I
was thirty-four years old and had no idea of what occupation
I might follow outside Africa.

CHAPTER SIX

I return to England and make an unsuccessful application – I am appointed Chief Constable of Chesterfield; then Chief Constable of the East Riding of Yorkshire – An unpleasant incident and an unpopular prosecution.

I APPLIED for leave and handed over to a Mr. Philip Mitchell. When next I saw him I was visiting Nairobi to discuss security; it was in 1947; I was representing M.I.5, and he had become Sir Philip Mitchell, Governor and Commander-in-Chief, Kenya.

It is possible that my resolve to leave Africa for good in 1922 was not even then absolute. But, virtually on the eve of our departure, I received a cable from Dollie's father, who was always greatly concerned for our welfare, and that cable contained a momentous suggestion. The post of Chief Constable of Hull had become vacant; did I not think I stood a chance of getting the appointment; if so, would I make my application right away and send it by cable? The idea appealed to me instantly, for surely here was the solution to all my problems—a police job in which at least some of my experience in Africa would prove valuable, and an appointment in England in Dollie's home town. I sent off my cabled application and then realized that we had hardly time to catch the only boat from Mombasa which would get me to England for the interview.

We managed it, however, by catching a *dhow* from Tanga. For me, owner of an imperturbable stomach, this trip by starlight in the little single-masted ship expertly navigated by Arabs was a romantic delight. But it was one of the rare times when Dollie and I did not see eye to eye. The combination of the violent rocking of our little craft and the perfectly appalling stench of the raw hides which were our cargo turned our picturesque voyage into a nightmare of sea-sickness for her—and also, incidentally, for Peter, our Airedale, who was not a good sailor either. They were both uninterested in my plans for the future by the time we arrived at Mombasa to catch the boat back to England.

I had, incidentally, the privilege of travelling home with my old G.O.C., for General Sir Edward Northey, who had formerly been G.O.C. Rhodesia and Nyasaland troops, was now retiring from the Governorship of Kenya, and was returning to England on that same boat.

My spirits were so high when we eventually reached Hull, that it never occurred to me that I might not get the job I had set my heart on. But this, to my great disappointment, was what happened. It was a sorry anti-climax to my dramatic dash across half the world, and it left me at something of a loss what to do next.

However, I had a few months' leave due to me and some money saved, and when I was introduced to my daughter Audrey, who was by now eighteen months old, I decided that by hook or by crook I must find a way to remain in England. There were several family conferences about what I should do and we decided that I should apportion my savings so that they would cover three years and spend that time reading for the Bar. Meanwhile, I would continue to look for a suitable job, but, if the worst came to the worst, I should at least be able at the end of my three years to return to East Africa and practise as a barrister. My kindly father-in-law, at whose house we were staying, listened to our long discussions without saying very much, but one morning at breakfast there was an envelope on my plate. It contained his cheque for £500 to meet my Bar expenses, and was one of the pleasantest surprises I have ever had.

I enrolled as a student of Gray's Inn, plodded along with my studies, and became increasingly depressed. I did not know quite what sort of job I ought to be looking for, but I knew that we should all be much more happy if I could find one. Then, towards the end of February 1923 Dollie and I went to Monkseaton to spend a few days with my mother and father. My mother had invited a neighbour and his wife to tea. I cannot to-day remember the names of these friends except that the man was called Reggie. I had never met either of them, and I have not seen them since. Indeed, I came near to not meeting them at all, for shortly before tea the phone rang. "I say, it's Reggie here," a voice said when I lifted the receiver. "My wife can't come this afternoon, I'm afraid." I pressed him to come on his own anyway, and this he did, and proved to be a very sympathetic listener as I related my worries about my future.

Suddenly he made a suggestion. He had seen in a news-paper that a new Chief Constable was needed for Chesterfield; why didn't I try for that? At first this seemed to me to be an occasion for hollow laughter. Had I not just proved that Chief Constableships were not for me? Reggie, however, though he had nothing whatsoever to do with the police and was prompted only by some unexpectedly kindly impulse, would not let the matter rest. He insisted on returning to his own house to find the newspaper. It turned out to be a week old—and when we read the notice we found that the last day applications could be accepted was that very one. I gave up immediately. To my mind, the matter was closed.

But the indomitable Reggie was not to be beaten so easily. "Ring up the Town Clerk," he commanded briskly, "and ex-plain the circumstances—he'll let you have an extra day."

Swept away on the tide of his enthusiasm, I did as he said, and my application was allowed. Much to my surprise I was in-vited to Chesterfield a few days afterwards—I was on the "short list" of final applicants. There were six of us, all the others experienced senior police officers.

The members of the Watch Committee heard me with admirable patience as I stated my qualifications for the job. The Chairman then asked: "Captain Sillitoe, what are you doing now?" I answered that I was reading for the Bar, but that, to be frank, I was in fact one of the unemployed.

This reply seemed to amuse them. And I was given the job. To the members of the Chesterfield Watch Committee, and also to the members of the Police Force there who subsequently supported me so lovally I shall always feel deeply grateful.

Thanks to them, I now had my chance to make a career for myself in England.

Police duties in a town like Chesterfield had many similarities, I was pleased to find, with those in towns like Salisbury and Bulawayo. There was not much wrong that could not be induced to yield to the persuasion of common sense, and few problems that the asking of a few pertinent questions could not solve.

However, I could not see how the police of Chesterfield could be expected to carry out their duties with pride and dignity when their headquarters and offices, which were part of the court itself, were so inadequate in size and so dingy. My first decision was to ask the Watch Committee to authorize the building of new police offices, a new fire station, and a system of electric fire-alarm posts on the main street corners. My own contribution to the cost of this was to persuade many of the surrounding local authorities to pay Chesterfield a retaining fee for the services, in case of need, of the fire brigade. I also busied myself with reorganizing the police force on what I felt were more efficient lines.

They were very decent fellows, the first British police with whom I had any intimate contact, and I was deeply impressed. The job at Chesterfield reawakened all my old enthusiasm for police work.

When two years later the Standing Joint Committee of the East Riding of Yorkshire, with police headquarters at Beverley, advertised for a new Chief Constable, I applied for this job. It had what I considered to be two very big attractions. First the salary was £750 a year and, secondly, there was a very handsome house in the country that went with the appointment. By this time I needed a larger house, for my son Anthony had been born in January 1924.

I had rather a touching experience during my last few days at Chesterfield. I attended a newsboys' annual treat, and made a little speech. I told them they had conducted themselves very well during the year, and I took the opportunity of wishing one young man, from whom I bought my nightly newspaper, much happiness in his recent marriage.

When I had finished, another young newspaper seller stood up and said the newsboys had heard I was going to leave Chesterfield, and they all wanted him to say for them how sorry they were, and to wish me luck in my new job. They gave me three cheers, and I valued that tribute very much.

When I got to Beverley I found almost at once that there were drawbacks in this new job. The East Riding of Yorkshire was a singularly peaceful and law-abiding community. There were practically no law-breakers at all except for an occasional drunk or poacher. The Chief Constable was expected to enjoy himself and lead the life of a country gentleman, and during the shooting season I could have shot for six days of every week, for all the work I had to do.

Lord Deramore—the Lord Lieutenant of the County—put the position quite reasonably. "If there is work to do, Sillitoe, you will of course do it, but otherwise we shall be glad to see you in the hunting field, and if, by the way, you are out of the county for more than three weeks, you might just let me know."

This post could have been most enjoyable if I had possessed a private income. But we needed three maids to run the handsome house that had so attracted me, and we had two children. Even in 1925 fifteen pounds a week did not stretch far enough to allow me to hunt as well.

Then an unpleasant incident occurred. One of my constables, a typical good-natured, simple-hearted country policeman, was patrolling the King's highway upon his lawful occasions, and arrived at twelve noon at Blanch Farm Gate on the North Dalton road. The date was September 25th, and the shooting season had begun. P.C. Parker's simple instruction was to be at Blanch Farm Gate at noon, and wait five minutes. This was a fairly common sort of patrol instruction to country policemen in days before radio cars and easy telephone communication. It was the only way a duty sergeant could hope to keep any track of where his men were, when they were scattered over an area as wide and rural as the Yorkshire Ridings.

Next afternoon two documents arrived upon my desk. One was from Col. the Hon. Guy Wilson, C.M.G., D.S.O., of

Market Harborough, son of the Dowager Lady Nunburn-holme, and himself a local magistrate. He protested to me that one of my constables had interfered with the enjoyment of himself and his shooting party; and that, when spoken to, the fellow had been insolent, and that he—Col. the Hon. Guy Wilson—wanted to be sure that this constable was taught a sharp lesson, given a severe reprimand, and, in other words, instructed to respect the landed gentry.

The other document was a long report written painstakingly, and in obvious deep anxiety, by the constable himself. I will quote this report from P.C. Parker, because it seems to be a very human and significant document.

"Sir, I am stationed at Huggate, and on September 25th at about 12 noon, I arrived at Blanch Farm Gate on the North Dalton Road, where I was due at that time in the course of my duty. When I reached this point I observed a number of men coming from a stubble field from Blanch Farm. I was in uniform, and standing near the gatepost, which is directly on the road. I saw the men 150 yards away, and came to the con-clusion that it was Col. Wilson, as I knew the head keeper who was with him. Col. Wilson came out of the field, and as he approached me I saluted him and said, 'Good morning, sir.' Col. Wilson came right up to me and said, 'Don't you think it's damned foolish standing there like a big silly ass. I might have shot you!'

"I replied, 'I beg your pardon, sir, but to whom are you speaking?' Col. Wilson said, 'You, of course.' I replied: 'In the first place, do not speak to me in that manner, sir, as I am here in the execution of my duty, and such duty compels me to be here at the present time.' Col. Wilson replied: 'Rot, you have a beat, why don't you keep on it,' and indicating the road to North Dalton, said, 'There is a mile or two of straight road down there, you should have gone down it and got out of my way.' I pointed out to him that I was there in the execution of my duty, and was obliged to be there at a certain time. Col. Wilson said, 'Are you tied to the damned gatepost?'

"I replied, 'I am at present, Sir, and for the time being intend to stay here.'

"Col. Wilson then said to me: 'I think you talk like a damned fool.' He was standing about two yards away from me, as he spoke. The head keeper, Mr. England, was standing near to Col. Wilson and the other keepers were in close proximity.

"Col. Wilson then passed behind me and entered the turnip field. At that time I was not certain who he was, but I had a good idea, and checked with one of the two keepers who followed him."

I perfectly understood the Colonel's irritation, but to my way of thinking, my constable was doing his best to perform his duty, and that was to do what he had been told and not to take the law into his own hands and make changes in the routine that had been set him, in order to fall in with the whims of any citizen, no matter what his position in local society. In a police job, discipline is extremely important, as it is in the Army, and I had no intention of reprimanding a conscientious man for insisting on performing the work that had been set him according to the instructions he had received.

I went to see Lord Deramore, and told him that I proposed to take police proceedings against the Hon. Guy Wilson, if he would approve. Lord Deramore agreed, but said that Wilson ought first to be given an opportunity to withdraw his offensive remarks, and to apologize to the constable. This seemed reasonable, and I must say that I fully expected this was what he would do.

Instead, he denied the incident and wrote to me that there was no word of truth in my constable's story.

At Pocklington Petty Sessions he was summoned to answer charges of using abusive language; using abusive language with intent to put a person in fear; using abusive language so as to occasion a breach of the peace; and using abusive language to a police constable.

So this case became a *cause célèbre*, for my reaction was considered by many of the local aristocracy to indicate a most amazing attitude on the part of the Chief Constable. Why on earth, they argued, should I prefer to take the side of a country policeman rather than that of a titled land owner?

I had instructed a local solicitor, Mr. Harry Wray, to conduct the case for the police. Wilson had briefed a London barrister, Mr. Tristan Beresford, instructed by London solicitors.

I had asked Mr. Wray to express how very much I, as Chief Constable, regretted having to apply for the summons to be issued. Mr. Wray, in opening, explained that the first of the charges was brought under the East Riding County Council by-law, and the fourth charge under a very old by-law which was still in existence. He read the correspondence which had passed between Col. Wilson and myself, in which Col. Wilson denied the charges, and explained that I had asked Col. Wilson to give an unqualified apology to the policeman, and had received a reply from his solicitors that their client could not withdraw anything he had not said.

Constable Parker took the witness box nervously, and gave his evidence in very much the same words as the report he had submitted to me. He added, in reply to Mr. Wray's questions, that to a certain extent he had been in fear, and was wavering whether he should go away from his post of duty or remain.

Parker was cross-examined. "Did you serve in the war?"— "No, sir." "How old are you?" "I am twenty-three, sir." "Were you concerned with this shooting party?" "No, sir."

It was apparent to me that whatever the outcome of this case, the unfortunate Constable Parker was never again going to be able to patrol his rural beat in quite the same spirit of pastoral placidity as had marked his dutiful footsteps before.

He explained about the Blanch Farm Gate being his duty post for twelve noon on this day in question, and admitted— for what it was worth—that he could see a mile down the road, and that he was quite conspicuous in that part of the roadway.

Yes, he had his bicycle. Yes, he could have gone 100 or 150 yards further down the road. No, he did not think he was silly in standing there at his duty station.

The purpose of the cross-examination at this point seemed to me to be based on the contention that a police constable on the highway should have realized it was his duty to move out of the way of the guns of a shooting party which was approaching him across a field, rather than that the sportsmen should withhold their fire for the safety of the person on the road-way.

Nobody in court seemed to think this contention remarkable.

Constable Parker agreed that the beaters were spread about the field, and that he saw two hares get up, but no one shot at them. The hares did not come his way.

The point of the cross-examination was still the same—what was Constable Parker doing on the King's highway at a point where he might be interfering with the private pastimes of Col. the Hon. Guy Wilson, C.M.G., D.S.O.?

When asked: "Did you not feel that you might have been in physical danger?" Constable Parker replied: "The only danger that I could see was in not doing my duty right, by being anywhere but at my duty post."

The next question was: "I put it to you that you have been taught your evidence and have had to learn it by heart." Constable Parker, reasonably enough, denied this imputation.

Col. Guy Wilson, in the witness box, said he lived at Market Harborough and on the day in question was shooting on the Warter estate belonging to his mother, and was coming across the field with five or six keepers, or it might have been seven, when he saw the constable about half a mile away. They put up a covey of partridges, but he did not shoot for fear of hitting the constable. He thought he had one shot when the birds got out of the constable's line. He came out of the gateway with the head keeper. He thought they were all there, but found out later that the rest were some distance away, and did not hear what took place when he approached the constable.

He said that he had received a letter from the Chief Constable, and replied to it in a day or two, and to the best of his knowledge wrote exactly what he thought was true, stating that he appreciated the constable's duty, but it was not very intelligently carried out. "When speaking to the constable," he continued, "I did not say 'damned silly ass', and certainly the words 'silly ass' were not used. I think I said 'that particular' or 'that very gatepost', and I never called the constable a 'bloody fool'. I have been in command of men and do not gesticulate and am not in the habit of shouting. I was most anxious to have this charge dealt with and that was why I wrote to the Chief Constable to deal with it—or I would deal with it myself, for I took a very serious view of the aspersions upon me."

He was, he said, absolutely clear in his own mind that he did not use any offensive remarks. The constable was never in any danger, but might have been had he, the Colonel, been stupid enough to fire. The constable undoubtedly interfered with the game crossing the road into the turnips.

Cross-examined, he agreed that he was "rather put out" when he was crossing the stubble. The constable did say he was there in the execution of his duty and had to be there. In his opinion he thought the constable could have gone a little way down the road and still have been fulfilling his duty, but he ended up by saying that if it was his duty to be there he had no more to say. On his oath he did not use the words "damned gatepost", and he did not use the word "bloody". He certainly used the word "damned". He did not ask Ben to convey his regret to the constable for his offence. The word "damned" was not abusive. If he had never written the letter to the Chief Constable he would not have been there now. On 1st October he sent a denial of the whole of the report to the Chief Constable.

Benjamin Wilson England, the head keeper of Warter Priory, was called by the defence to corroborate his employer's statements, and stated he heard all that passed between the Colonel and the constable, and there was not a single offensive word used. Col. Wilson was not a gentleman given to using bad language, and did not gesticulate. The constable was equally civil. He met the constable near Kilnwick Percy Vicarage on the day of the dog trials, and said to him, "I hope you are not making anything of that silly case, and shall be sorry if you have to report," and the constable replied that he had sent a report in. He never said to the constable, "the boss was a bit hot with you."

Mr. Beresford, in addressing the Bench, said that the case was of the greatest importance to Col. Wilson, in that it cast aspersions upon him in his position as a Justice of the Peace. He contended that if Col. Wilson had been prepared to withdraw something he had not said, the case would never have been brought, but the Colonel had such a strong feeling in the matter that he had gone to considerable expense and trouble and was perfectly justified in bringing the case forward to clear himself from these allegations. The Bench, he hoped, would notice the long delay that had been shown in answering Col. Wilson's first letter, and that it was only after a second letter stating that Col. Wilson was likely to take steps himself that the reply and the constable's report were sent. He produced extracts from the Oxford Dictionary bearing on the meaning of the words "bloody" and "damned", showing that the words were in no way "obscene" or "abusive", and asked the Bench to dismiss the case and allow Col. Wilson to leave the court without a stain upon his honour.

The Bench made a brief adjournment, and then returned to announce that they had unanimously decided to dismiss all the charges.

So that was that, and if I had previously acquired any popularity with the landed gentry of Yorkshire's East Riding, it was in doubt from that day onwards.

Anyway, I had already made up my mind to leave the county whenever I had the chance, as I simply could not afford to stay there, particularly as my family had increased again, for in November 1925 my second son, Richard, was born. When I saw that the City of Sheffield was advertising for a Chief Constable, at a salary of £1,000 a year, rising to £1,250, I applied for the post at once. I knew little about Sheffield except that I had visited there on one or two occasions when I was Chief Constable of Chesterfield, but I felt sure that whatever else I might find in Sheffield, there would at least be plenty of hard work, and that I should be required to administer only the actual statutory and common law of good citizenship, and not feel myself responsible for the unwritten code of behaviour that might exist between country squire and villager.

CHAPTER SEVEN

I become Chief Constable of Sheffield – The Sheffield gangs and our measures for dealing with them.

I FIRMLY believed that the man who would get the job of Chief Constable of Sheffield would be Mr. Barker, the Assistant Chief, who had a splendid record. The newspapers, however, seemed, for some reason that I have never understood, to favour my own chances, and devoted considerable space to photographs of me and details of my career.

Their insight proved to be correct. I was chosen for the appointment and was most touchingly and sincerely congratulated by Mr. Barker. There had been fifty-three applicants for the post, and I considered myself very lucky indeed to have got it.

My colleagues of the East Riding police gave me a gold watch, an illuminated address, and a farewell smoking concert. The Guy Wilson affair had, it seemed, made a tremendous impression on the entire force. Until this case was brought, some of the landed gentry had tended to regard the village policeman as a servant. It was not only in the East Riding, but fairly common throughout most English rural areas, that the constable would find himself posted for duty to places where he could best be of service to the landowner, as a kind of uniformed gamekeeper.

The prosecution by me of Col. Wilson had been perhaps the first real indication to the East Riding force that there were chief constables who were prepared not only to stand by them, but also to regard the police officer as entitled to the respect of every citizen, no matter whom. I had failed in court in the prosecution, but I was encouraged—and deeply moved—to discover that I had succeeded in raising the morale of my force by taking my stand. That was the important thing.

The police problems of Sheffield, I quickly discovered, were very different from the rural clashes of the East Riding of Yorkshire. Here, in this busy city, the only class distinction was between honest citizens and criminals—and there were plenty of the latter, for Sheffield was at this time in the grip of its notorious gangs.

I took over my duties in Sheffield on the 1st May 1926—the first day of the General Strike. Every worker in the Corporation Transport Department had walked out. A few private coach companies kept on operating, however, and it was not long before the trams were running, with adventure-hungry young university students as drivers and conductors. This at once roused the ire of the strikers and clashes were frequent.

There were attempts to overturn the vehicles. Stones were thrown and windows smashed. Innocent passengers were injured, drivers and conductors were assaulted, and strikers were, of course, hurt too. The leaders seemed determined to address their rallies and mass meetings at the most inconvenient spots in Sheffield—such as the main square outside the town hall, and indeed at every other strategic, but from my point of view awkward, place.

I must confess that I had considerable sympathy with the strikers. I felt that the strike was wrong, but I could understand only too painfully well how unemployment, with all its hardships and humiliations, had affected the labour market until employers had in many cases dropped wages and made working conditions that indicated more thought for profits than for humanity.

Yet it was a strike, and it was our job to handle it. Troublemakers had to be arrested, and rowdy assemblies had to be broken up. I saw more police officers injured by the stones and sticks of strikers than there were casualties among the demonstrators themselves.

I do not believe that the majority of the strikers were wholeheartedly in favour of the drastic action their leaders had taken. Many hundreds of them came to offer themselves for duty as Special Constables, and three hundred were recruited and sent on duty in the streets during the first four days of the strike. I think it was significant also that the tram and bus service was operating within half an hour of the news reaching Sheffield that the General Strike was officially finished.

One of the big leaders of the strike in Sheffield was Councillor Frank Thraves, who was local secretary of the Passenger Transport branch of the Transport and General Workers' Union. His office was only a few yards from police headquarters, and Councillor Thraves was constantly visiting us to complain about the police interfering with strike demonstrations and marches. We got to know each other quite well.

The following November the Labour Party gained control of the Sheffield City Council and Thraves, who later became Alderman F. Thraves, C.B.E., J.P.—perhaps because the frequency with which he had dropped in on us had given him some sympathy with our activities!—was made chairman of the Sheffield Watch Committee. It might have been an inconvenient situation, but, as it happened, Alderman Thraves proved to be a very good friend of the police. He was most active in his insistence upon improved conditions of service for police officers and upon new stations and recreational facilities. I was keen on all these things myself, and we got along splendidly.

But the finish of the General Strike did not mean a return to normal police duties. The strike had been in support of the miners, and when everybody else went back to work, the miners remained out. This dragged on for many weary months, and Sheffield was badly affected as three collieries were shut down, and coal was badly needed for the local steel works. Inevitably, "outcropping" for domestic use started on a very large scale, and once again the police had to interfere to prevent, not only damage to property, but the risk of men digging inside shallow tunnels that were in almost every case without timbered supports. I went along personally to these outcrop sites and chatted informally with the men who were digging in them. I warned them that it was illegal to remove the coal, and pointed out the risks they ran of being injured by falls. They nearly all appreciated my personal warnings—realizing, perhaps, how easy it would have been for me to have stayed in my office and sent officers to arrest them. The outcropping gradually stopped without any serious incidents of any kind.

To help the strikers occupy their spare time, and to raise funds for them, we arranged many football matches between them and the police. These were all played with gratifying good will, and when the strike eventually finished I was glad to be able to look back upon it as an interlude that, although difficult, had ended without any serious clashes.

I was now able to concentrate upon the problems of Sheffield's gangs, which had flourished during the strike even better than before. They had organized a big open-air gambling game in the Park district of Sheffield, and many of the men who had been forced into idleness frequented it. The game played was "tossing", and it was done with five half-crowns, the betting being upon the proportion of "heads" to "tails". The assemblies were illegal, but it was difficult to break them up, for the Park areas were desolate open spaces, and long before the police could approach, they were spotted by "look-outs" and the gamesters broke up and ran for it. The evidence was easily disposed of by putting the five half-crowns into the "croupier's" trousers pocket with his other loose change.

The gang leader who controlled the "tossing ring" at this time was George Mooney, chief of the Mooney Gang; but, because it was a very enviable source of income, the members of the Garvin Gang coveted it, and were already beginning to skirmish and fight for its possession.

These two gangs, both named after their leaders, had virtually complete control of the poorer districts of Sheffield. Each gang had hundreds of members, and they were almost unchecked in their villainies. They had no hesitation about swarming around a police officer and attacking him if he tried to interfere with their betting or other criminal activities, whether upon the wastelands of the Park district, or among the drab back streets around it, or in Crofts and Norfolk Bridge areas.

In 1926, these three districts were, without any doubt, as rough and lawless as any to be found in England. The pub-

Taking over from the late Supt. Robson
of East Riding, 1925

Chief Constable of Sheffield. A cartoon
from the *Yorkshire Telegraph and Star*,
19th October 1928

With velvet gloves on iron hands
He keeps the peace in all our borders,
But on no ceremony stands
With those who flout him or his orders.

Glasgow, 1932.
The first police radio-van

'Big Tommy'—Sgt. Morrison
of the Glasgow Constabulary

licans and shopkeepers lived in daily terror of the Mooney and Garvin Gangs, for—when they were not in the tossing ring, or thieving and fighting among themselves—one of their favourite pastimes was robbing public houses.

They would split into "raiding parties" of four or five men and walk into a public house, leaving one man outside. The men who walked into the pub ordered whiskies and cigarettes. They didn't offer to pay, but drained their glasses, pocketed their cigarettes and announced: "We're the Mooney Boys." If the landlord still demanded payment, they promptly flung their emptied glasses at the big mirror behind the bar and began to smash bottles and glasses, to kick the furniture to pieces, to wreck the beer pumps and beer barrels, and to throw the hapless landlord to the floor, should he attempt to interfere. Then they would depart and, while the gasping victim was staggering to his feet to call the police, the fifth man would walk in and say in tones of awe: "Those were some of Mooney's gangsters—very dangerous fellows! If you complain to the police they'll be sure to come back and give you some more. The Mooney boys aren't afraid of the police."

This was regrettably quite true. The Mooney boys were not afraid of the police, nor were the Garvin boys. There existed at this time no reason why they should have been, for if a police officer, despite peril of disfigurement and brutal attack, was valiant enough to arrest any of them, there was not much satisfaction to be gained in Sheffield's magistrates' courts, for witnesses were afraid to speak for the prosecution. The gangs fought each other, and a slashed or beaten gangster would not bear testimony against his enemy. Nor would the publicans, nor the other inhabitants of these pitiful grey streets. They preferred to suffer in silence the wrong that was done to them, rather than risk further and yet more terrible vengeance.

This was the biggest difficulty. Unfortunately, also, one or two of the lay magistrates admitted to me that they themselves were, frankly, afraid of the Mooney and Garvin gangsters.

I called my senior officers together and asked them to select very carefully for me some of the strongest, hardest-hitting men under their commands. I had 700 policemen, each with a minimum chest measurement of thirty-six inches and height of five feet ten inches, all fit and healthy men, and none of them was disinclined to play the gangsters at their own game and meet violence with the strong arm of the law.

It was not difficult to pick a dozen of the best of these, to form a "flying squad" specially to deal with the gangster problem. These men were taught ju-jitsu and various other methods of attack and defence, and it was surprising how little teaching they needed. They had just been waiting for the chance to learn!

They soon divided themselves into little teams—usually pairs—for patrol work in the notorious gangster districts. One of the most famous of these teams was that of "Loxley and Lunn". Loxley was six feet three inches tall and weighed eighteen stone. There was not an ounce of soft flesh on him. He was granite hard, and to hit him, even with boxing gloves, was like striking a brick wall. Jerry Lunn was not quite so tall, but was a beautifully balanced man who could hit like the kick of a mule. As they walked down the streets together they looked like a battleship with its attendant destroyer. And they were staunch friends. Both had a fierce contempt for the "cowardly little gangster rats", as they always called the Garvin and Mooney mobsters.

Sergt. Robinson and a giant Irishman named Geraghty made another celebrated "flying squad" team. Geraghty was the only man I have ever known who could not merely hold seven tennis balls in one fist, but could actually pick up five loose tennis balls in one hand.

I called a meeting of the publicans who were being most frequently victimized by the gangsters. I told them about my plans. I said: "I have picked some of my officers, and am going to put them in plain clothes. Their job will be to patrol the pubs and streets of your districts. If they come to your public houses, they will make themselves known to you and will then sit quietly and wait. If these gangs of thugs arrive and there is any disorderliness or attempts at intimidation, all you have to do is to say to my men that you want these people removed from your premises, as they are creating a disturbance. If my men are not there, you can telephone for them to be sent down and they will be with you in less than ten minutes."

I told my men—not merely those of the flying squad, but also the entire force—that in any of their dealings with known gangsters and bullies I would stand by them whatever happened.

I sent for Sam Garvin and George Mooney, and gave them both a stern warning. I said: "From now on you must understand that you and your kind are an offence to decent citizens. If you see a police officer you had better get out of his sight. If any of my officers are put in the dock for hammering you, I shall be in the dock with them!"

Then, having delivered fair warning, I sent the "flying squad" into action and the cases began to flow into court. The charge was usually "disorderly conduct AND assaulting the police".

When the gangsters were brought to the court, I always made it my business to attend the trials, and after the hooligans had been convicted, the prosecuting solicitor would ask permission for me to enter the witness-box. There, upon oath, I would give evidence as Chief Constable of the City, about the menace of these gangs and the frequency of such offences, and ask for exemplary punishment. By doing this I took the weight of responsibility from the magistrates and let it fall upon my own shoulders. The results were good.

There was a typical case, for instance, of a gangster named Foster. He was a "razor king", and carried a razor blade stuck into a bit of wood hidden up his sleeve and fixed to a length of elastic. On the least pretext he would pluck the razor blade down from his sleeve and use it mercilessly. He had several convictions for assaulting and slashing people, and had been merely fined each time. The more convictions he got the greater he was held in fear, and the quicker his fine was paid for him. He had developed a contempt for authority that was hardly surprising.

One night there was trouble at a licensed house in West Bar. Loxley and Lunn strode in. One of the men there was Foster, and as soon as he saw Loxley he jumped at him with the razor flashing.

He was promptly seized with "reasonable force" and removed from West Bar to the police charge office, a distance of 200 yards. The desk-sergeant refused to accept the charge until Foster had been treated at the infirmary. He was charged with being drunk and disorderly and assaulting P.C. Loxley.

Next day I was in court. The public gallery was crowded with Mooney gangsters. As soon as the proceedings began, Foster's solicitor stood up and said he objected to the charge. He cast a significant glance at huge P.C. Loxley and then at the figure of his bandaged and cowed client in the dock and said solemnly: "I wish to have the charge amended, your worship, from 'assaulting the police' to one of 'attempted suicide'."

There was a howl of laughter in which all the gangsters in the public gallery heartily joined, and I remember that even the magistrates permitted themselves to smile.

But the flying squad proved to be no laughing matter for the Sheffield gangsters. It came eventually to the point that when a couple of these policemen entered a public house any gangsters present would remove themselves without waiting to be asked, leaving their drinks unfinished.

Some people may have considered this to be an "unconstitutional" way of handling the problem. Yet until it was handled by these means, the dark lanes, courts, and by-ways of the East End and centre of Sheffield were unsafe places for respectable citizens after dark. These gangsters carried razors, knives, coshes, and similar hideous implements. They showed absolutely no hesitation about using them. Frequently, victims were taken to the infirmary terribly injured. But the gangsters had spread such terror that the injured victim would rarely be persuaded to come voluntarily to court and testify. They—and any eye-witnesses—had always to be subpœnaed. I never knew any gangster to protest against the way the police handled him, even in the more serious cases which went to the Assize Court in Leeds—though pleas were sometimes submitted by defence counsel to the Grand Jury at the Assize Court that police brutality had occurred. The attitude of the average citizen was never more clearly manifested than by the action of these Grand Juries, who never failed, after careful and fair investigation, to dismiss the accusations as being completely without foundation, and to uphold the charges against the gangsters.

This success was the beginning of my own reputation, and I have often been referred to since as "the man who broke the Sheffield gangs". The truth was that the Sheffield gangs were broken by the courageous police of Sheffield, on the battle-grounds of the open streets, and in the calm atmosphere of the law courts. The police were only too eager and happy to tackle this unsavoury and risky job once they were shown the way. By the standards of gangland, my officers were unarmed, for the flying squad relied almost entirely upon good physique and did not often deign to use even the diminutive official "detective batons", which are only about two-thirds the length of a uniformed constable's truncheon, and were their sole weapon against the savage knives and coshes of the Mooney and Garvin gangs. My attitude was that if you threaten a man with a razor you cannot complain should he thereupon knock you down with his fists.

I believe that there is only one way to deal with the gangster mentality. You must show that you are not afraid. If you stand up to them and they realize that you mean business, they will soon knuckle under. The element of beast in a man, whether it comes from an unhappy and impoverished background, or from his own undisciplined lustful appetites, will respond exactly as a wild beast of the jungle responds—to nothing but greater force and greater firmness of purpose.

The Mooney and Garvin gangs had a final clash, as a result of which both leaders were sent to prison. After George Mooney came out, when his sentence was completed, I sent for him and saw him alone in my private office. I spoke to him like a father. I said: "Well, Mooney, you see what my attitude is. If you chaps do this sort of thing I am going to see that you go to prison, and it's not getting you anywhere. Now, what is the sense of it?"

Mooney did not answer. I went on: "Why don't you stop

this damned nonsense of fighting Sam Garvin's men? I shall stamp out his gang just as I shall stamp out yours, but if you have any decency in you, as I believe you have, you won't wait to be wiped out like some sort of dirty pestilence. You will come to your senses while there is time and keep your dignity."

When he got up to leave I said: "I really believe you will try to better yourself, Mooney, and I want to shake you by the hand."

He stood and looked at my proffered hand for a long moment without saying a word. As I was about to withdraw it, he burst suddenly into tears, grasped it and said: "You are the first gentleman I have ever had the privilege of shaking hands with, sir."

I shall never forget the sight of George Mooney, gang leader of such terrifying reputation, grasping my hand as his face worked like an emotional child's. Happily he became—and remained—one of Sheffield's respectable citizens.

It is only fair to admit that I tried an identical technique with Sam Garvin, without getting much result. Garvin did not have it in him to respond to such treatment. If there was any spark of decency there, it needed more than a kind word and a proffered handshake to fan it into any visible flame. So we took the only course left to us and simply harassed him off the streets of Sheffield.

CHAPTER EIGHT

My first meeting with Dr. Webster – The beginnings and development of the forensic laboratory at Sheffield – An early demonstration of the value of scientific evidence.

ON Easter Monday of 1924, at the Anchor Inn at Whittington Moor, near Chesterfield, a man had taken an axe and attacked the woman who was the object of his affections. She was gravely injured and near to death when the police found her. There was not much masterly sleuthing involved in the case. The man was arrested, taciturn and blood-splashed, with his unmistakable finger-prints dabbled generously over the axe handle.

The woman was moved to the town hospital and lay unconscious for several days. It was, of course, imperative that the police should seek to obtain a statement from her as soon as possible, but days passed and still my C.I.D. officers had not produced this statement. I asked what the trouble was, and they told me, ruefully, that there was a tartar of a resident surgeon at the hospital, a young Scottish doctor named Webster, who would not let them near the woman. The detective concerned with the case had pleaded and argued, but it was unavailing.

When I went along to the hospital myself, I was told that Dr. Webster was too busy to see anybody. I decided to wait. At last, along the hospital corridor came the young Scots doctor. He was just as he had been described to me, of stocky build, his hair untidy, and with a general appearance of having slept in his clothes. He probably had, for I afterwards found out that he had stayed night and day with the injured woman, fighting for her life—which, incidentally, he did eventually save, thus sparing her assailant from having to face a charge of murder, and allowing him to get off with a sentence of hard labour for violent assault.

I was leaning rather wearily against the wall for I had been waiting a long time. I said, politely, "Excuse me, Doctor, but how is Mrs. So-and-so?" He looked me up and down, then growled uncompromisingly, "And who the hell are you?" I said, with what I hoped was ingratiating modesty, "I'm no-body—just the Chief Constable." He continued to glare, apparently unimpressed. Then: "Oh well, if you're the Chief Constable I suppose you had better come into the kitchen for a cup of tea."

That was how I met the man who was to become Professor James M. Webster—in my opinion one of the most brilliant pathologists in Britain to-day. If Professor Webster had worked in London at Scotland Yard, he would, I am sure, have earned as great a reputation as did Sir Bernard Spilsbury. At present he is, of course, head of the West Midland Forensic Science Laboratory in Birmingham.

Before we had finished our cups of tea, perched on uncomfortable wooden chairs in the little hospital kitchen, we were firm friends. The friendship was an unexpected one, yet it has proved sincere and lasting.

Eventually he took me to see the woman he had so carefully guarded. She was still unconscious, and it was apparent why he had not permitted my C.I.D. officers to intrude upon her. I was immensely impressed by the care and interest he took in his patient. He seemed to have surrounded her with every ingenious medical device that a small town hospital could hope to provide.

"She is very badly injured," he said quietly. "It isn't just axe wounds, either. See here"—he pointed to a fading bruise—"the fellow kicked her there, and this"—he indicated another faint mark—"was probably a blow from his fist." He explained the difference between the wounds made by axe blows when the woman was standing up and those she had received when lying on the ground; also the different marks of the bruises made by fist and those made by axe handle.

I was impressed and rather excited. Forensic science as we know it to-day was only in its infancy in 1924, and even fingerprints were a comparatively new science then. In the years that followed after I left Chesterfield the thought struck me that the right kind of medical expert working in close collaboration with the police could prove of great value in the scientific detection of crime, particularly in cases of violence and murder.

Then, in Sheffield, I was able to develop my ideas about the forensic side of provincial police work, for I had the full support of the Watch Committee. My first move was to ask for a full-time police surgeon. This was certainly justified, for at that time I had seven hundred men and, as I pointed out to the Committee, every extra day of sickness caused by my men having to wait for attention from a doctor occupied with many other patients, was a disaster in our war against crime. I also guessed that if only I could get a doctor who was interested in the development of a forensic science laboratory of our own in Sheffield, he would contrive to find enough time for that too.

The Watch Committee agreed, and the vacancy for the post of Police Surgeon was advertised. To my surprise and delight, one of the candidates was Dr. J. M. Webster, the young Scot from Chesterfield. I had not seen or heard of him since I left there, but I unhesitatingly recommended his appointment, and he began work as my police surgeon on 1st April, 1929. He never tires of declaring that this was a profoundly significant date for him.

His duties included looking after not only the police force, but also—since the Watch Committee, however amiable, insisted on having its money's worth—the fire brigade, and anyone who happened to be held in custody in the police cells pending trial.

He was also to devote such time as he could reasonably spare to analytical work and post-mortems of persons whose deaths, *prima facie*, were not due to natural causes. I told him I would give him all the help I could, and we soon had a very promising little forensic laboratory built up. It began in a small way, conducting examinations of stains on clothing, in, for instance, cases of carnal knowledge or rape. It could not be claimed that this laboratory was the first of its kind in the country, for its development was taking place side by side with similar work in Nottingham under Captain Athelstan Popkess, but it is certainly true to say that the police forces of Nottingham and Sheffield anticipated by years the police laboratory at Hendon, serving Scotland Yard. Derby County had the first policeman scientist, in the person of Supt. Else, who was, I believe, the first man in England to give evidence regularly on the analysis of soils, feathers, and so on, in the police prosecutions typical of his rural district. That was as early as 1928.

Formerly, the scientific investigation of crime had been virtually a monopoly in the hands of Spilsbury, Wilcox, and Roche Lynch, whose services were in constant pressing demand and whose fees were correspondingly high. When none of these three specialists was available to assist a police force, there was nobody else. Nottingham, Sheffield, and Derby County represented the first systematic breakaway from this sometimes autocratic monopoly.

I had the idea of circulating some of the neighbouring forces about our plans, and rather doubtfully approached Dr. Webster to see how he felt about tackling extra work. To my delight he was very enthusiastic, realizing that the more jobs he worked on, the better the claim that could be made for extra apparatus in his forensic laboratory. Soon the little pioneer laboratory at Sheffield was serving Chesterfield, the West Riding, Doncaster, and Derby County. Before long we were undertaking forensic examinations of fibres, wood, safe-ballast (the powder that spills from a safe when it is being forced by thieves); examinations of blood, human stains, forcible entry scratches; and analyses of materials used in counterfeit coins, notes, and poison pen letters. I also set up a photographic department and fingerprint section supervised by Sergeant Hammond, assisted by a young police officer, Edward Burgess, who took over the work when Hammond left to join me later on in Glasgow.

I managed to persuade the Sheffield Watch Committee to finance the purchase of some very expensive photomicrography apparatus, an expenditure which soon paid for itself. Photomicrography became an important part of the laboratory work, and our apparatus served not only Sheffield, but the surrounding police forces as well. We followed this with ultra-violet ray lamps for detection of forgeries and concealed stains, and built a small animal house for keeping guinea pigs and rabbits for experimental purposes.

Webster also pointed out that we had no refrigeration plant at the mortuary, and this was installed at a cost of some £500. Previously, as various people informed us, it had been an unnecessarily distressing experience for relatives of a person who had met with a sudden death or who had died in suspicious circumstances, to be obliged to see the body after some time had elapsed while an inquiry was being conducted, and I should have considered the refrigeration plant indispensable if only to alleviate such distress. From the police point of view, however, there is other justification for this means of preserving bodies. For instance, in criminal cases it is sometimes stated by the defence that they have been unable to examine the body although the coroner or the police have requested a pathologist to make a post-mortem; but if the body has been properly preserved there is no reason why the defence should not have every facility to examine it, no matter how long a period of time elapses between the commission of the crime and the trial of the accused. Incidentally, still considering the matter from the point of view of the police, embalming, as commonly practised in the United States, is liable to hamper investigation rather than assist it, for the introduction of foreign fluids into the body obviously obscures the issue if a question of poisoning arises.

It was a great help to us that our little police laboratory, thanks to Dr. Webster, became allied with Sheffield University. Webster was appointed Lecturer in Toxicology and Forensic Medicine to the University in 1929. The result of this was that when we required assistance in any matter of advanced scientific nature, we had the willing co-operation of the entire University and the run of its lavishly equipped laboratories.

Professor Webster worked out a drill which made it a rule that whenever a major crime involved an offence against a person, i.e., murder or assault, the C.I.D. must disturb nothing until the police surgeon had inspected the scene of the crime, and photographs had been taken. I think we were the first police force in Britain to introduce this system, which is now a routine police drill everywhere; namely, that the pathologist, photographer, and plan-drawer are all on the scene of the crime—particularly of a murder—before anything is moved, so that officers specially trained in seeking details likely to be of scientific value can make a careful search for anything significant to them.

Before I left Sheffield, Professor Webster and I were to have the satisfaction of seeing the Home Office begin to take a keen interest in our system; and the Metropolitan Police agitated for the introduction of similar forensic laboratory facilities, although, of course, on a bigger scale, at Scotland Yard. I was asked by Mr. (later Sir Arthur) Dixon, Assistant Under-Secretary of State, Home Office, for a resumé of the working of our forensic science scheme in Sheffield, and I am told that when the "D" Committee, which was a sub-committee of the larger departmental board set up by the Home Office to consider methods of training detective officers in scientific investigation, began its work in 1931, a great deal of its material was based directly on the experiences we had had in Sheffield. The result was the publication of a handbook of instruction for all ranks of the country's police forces on the use of science in the detection and prevention of crime, and the setting up of the forensic science laboratories operating to-day.

Webster was concerned in one of the first cases to prove in a British court the value of scientific evidence. The case in question concerned a prize pig which had suddenly disappeared from its sty. Chesterfield C.I.D. interviewed several suspects and were getting no further until they called at the cottage of a man who seemed very anxious not to let them in. They persuaded him to let them search the cottage, but could find nothing incriminating; but when the police officer began to examine an old jacket hanging behind a door the suspect showed signs of agitation. There seemed to be nothing remarkable about it, however, except that the lining had been completely removed.

The officer took the jacket away and sent it to us at Sheffield to see if our laboratory could discover any clues in it. Among the fibres of hessian that had been used to pad the jacket shoulders, Professor Webster found traces of blood. The defence claimed this was human blood, but Webster was able to prove in court that it was the blood of a pig.

On another occasion a thief broke into several shops in Doncaster. One was a gunsmith's, and from this the thief stole a revolver wrapped in green baize. The only clue was a few wisps of thread that had been caught on the sky-light nail. A man was arrested, but stoutly denied knowledge of the offence. He had a badly withered arm, and it looked impossible for him to have accomplished the tricky climbing involved in these burglaries. It would certainly have been difficult to convince a jury that this cripple might be the culprit.

The suit of clothes in which he was arrested was sent to Professor Webster's laboratory. It was an ordinary-looking brown suit, yet when Webster had examined it he stated positively: "The man who wore this suit is the thief." In court he demonstrated that an apparently plain brown suit does in fact contain several colours in its weave. This particular suit had black, brown, and yellow threads that matched exactly with the threads discovered on the skylight nail.

To clinch his evidence, Professor Webster also described how he had found microscopic fragments of green baize in the right hand pocket of the suit where the thief had put the stolen pistol.

Webster was also one of the first police scientists to tackle the very controversial question of persons being "drunk in charge of a motor-car". Every responsible police officer is painfully aware that the system whereby a police surgeon visits the accused at the police station and makes him walk a chalked line, pick up coins, and do mental sums is unsatisfactory. If the accused person sends for his own doctor, as frequently happens, there is nearly always a prolonged bickering argument in court between the two medicos. This is bad, for it is only one man's opinion against another's whether the accused was drunk or not.

Sheffield, to the best of my belief, was the first police force in this country to adopt urine tests as regular routine in these cases, though investigation of blood-alcohol concentration and urine-alcohol concentration had already been made some time before, and such tests had become frequent in Denmark and Switzerland. An impetus was given to us in Sheffield by a modification of the chemical analysis by the late Dr. Southgate, then a Lecturer at Sheffield University. Chemical evidence was used not as a substitute for the clinical examination of motorists and the evidence of witnesses as to their manner of driving, but as an adjunct. Professor Webster and I always ensured that samples of urine or blood were never taken without the consent of the motorist, and the full test consisted of the chemical analysis not of one sample only but of two samples taken at an hour's interval; in this way there could be no fear of the tests being unfair or inconclusive.

Without having had any previous knowledge of scientific methods and their potential importance in my own line of country, I could see immediately that it was my duty to get every possible assistance for Webster in his work. Nothing was too good for the little laboratory that we started in Sheffield (it still exists, incidentally, and serves the Sheffield and Rotherham police forces to-day), and no matter what outlandish piece of costly equipment Professor Webster required, the Watch Committee provided it for him.

It was, by the way, during the time that Professor Webster and I were colleagues in Sheffield that we were both "black-balled". Webster, who, though an old St. Andrean, had not played golf for some years, agreed to take the game up again to keep me company. A friend of ours was most eager that we should join a club of which he was an official, and put our names up for membership. When the ballot was taken, however, the news had to be broken to us that we were not considered acceptable. We readily guessed why this was. Two notorious upholders of the law would be an embarrassment in a club where, as we later ascertained, the licensing laws were not infrequently violated and card games for fun only were the exception.

CHAPTER NINE

The policeman's lot – The importance of morale and my efforts to improve conditions in the Force – The introduction of police boxes and the recruitment of additional women police.

IN the years that I had spent in Chesterfield and then in the East Riding of Yorkshire, it had become apparent to me that no matter what personal brilliance a Chief Constable may possess, he can never succeed in his job unless he is able to ensure that the men under him are his willing and loyal colleagues, actively eager to co-operate with him. Obviously men with a grievance, men without incentive, or men with no sense of purpose in their work, who see themselves as meaningless cogs in a rather ungrateful machine, are never going to combine to make up a police force that is on its toes and a credit to its chief. So I was determined when I began work in Sheffield that whatever happened my men should be as contented as I could possibly make them. I had no doubt that any time and trouble I devoted to this object, and any expense which might be involved, would be amply repaid.

It is supremely important that men of integrity and enterprise should consider a police career sufficiently attractive to prefer it to others. And one has to remember that a great deal is asked of men who join the police. Every policeman lives, in a sense, a dedicated life—that may sound pretentious, but I believe it to be true. He cannot merely perform certain routine duties during duty hours and consider that he has fulfilled his obligations. On the contrary, he is never free to behave irresponsibly at any time—to get drunk, for instance, or indulge in the sort of escapades which most young men are attracted to occasionally, or to hang around with pals who, while being excellent company, may not be above a little dishonesty now and then. The policeman must remain circumspect at all times throughout his career for the simple reason that if he has a guilty secret he is in a vulnerable position and is liable to be blackmailed by those who know of his lapse and obliged by them to connive at their own misdoings.

Then, too, the police officer in this country has to remember that he is a symbol of law and justice to other citizens, and, as such, he cannot permit himself ordinary peccadilloes which could be easily forgiven in other people. For instance, I have always been most insistent that my officers should not drink before coming on duty, not for fear that they might be really drunk—obviously that would be intolerable—but because, in my opinion, a drink-cheery man, smelling strongly of alcohol, is not going to inspire confidence in—and may even be positively offensive to—those who may seek his aid, in, perhaps, an accident, or some other trouble or distress.

In the same way, if an ordinary citizen is provoked and loses his temper, that can be overlooked unless the consequences are unusually grave. It is, however, absolutely impermissible for an officer of the law to indulge in emotional outbursts of any kind. He must betray no personal animosity towards anyone, and his actions must on all occasions be compatible with his legal duty. For, once people began to suspect that policemen were capable of using their position to work off personal grudges or to gratify their own whims—whether kindly or petulant—the confidence which the public now feels in our police would be destroyed.

One small incident comes to my mind in this connection. It took place some years after my appointment in 1931 as Chief Constable of Glasgow City Police. The Hampden Park football ground in Glasgow was always packed with a tremendously excited crowd when international matches were being played, and the police often had a difficult job keeping order among the sometimes rather turbulent spectators. On this particular occasion, a wild Welsh supporter broke from the crowd and ran to try and fix a leek to the goal-post. A policeman went after him, of course, to persuade him to go back to his place, but the supporter decided to give the officer a run for his money. In the rather undignified chase which followed, the constable, made clumsy by his heavy boots, slipped and fell, and the crowd roared with laughter. Eventually, however, he caught his man. Now, I think most people would have felt pretty angry at having been made to look ridiculous in front of a huge assembly. But not for even an instant did his imperturbable good humour desert the constable, and as he marched his man off the field there was no vestige of personal annoyance and no violence in his attitude towards him. It was his duty to remove the man from the ground and to do it with the minimum force necessary; whatever his personal feelings were in the matter, he did not allow them to modify in the slightest his behaviour as an officer of the law. I must say that I felt that the prestige of the Glasgow Force had been tremendously enhanced by this constable's admirable self-control. The following day, I made a point of sending for him to tell him so.

It does not seem to me essential that a police constable should be a man of more than average intelligence or that he is necessarily going to be a better policeman if his standard of education is higher than the next man's. Indeed, I once argued with some passion on this point with Lord Trenchard. Trenchard was called upon by Ramsay MacDonald to deal with corruption in the Metropolitan Police Force and enhance its prestige in the early 1930's, after the case of the notorious Mrs. Meyrick and her illegal night clubs. It was his opinion that if university graduates could be induced to join the police force, improved standards of police conduct would automatically result. As an outcome of his belief the Hendon Police College was set up to be a staff college where university and public-school men—together with a small number of special entries of a high general standard of education—would be trained for three years to become an "officer" class in the police. These young men were to leave the college with the rank of Station Sub-Inspector. My view was—and still is—that the police force needs not exceptionally high standards of education, but very great integrity and strength of character, combined with the wisdom which comes to some—though not all—men when they have had wide and varied practical experience of human nature. To me, it seemed absurd that these young men should be sent out as the superiors of Superintendents twice their age who often had a great fund of real knowledge acquired through their years of service, and who were now, as a result of this scheme, debarred from any chance of promotion beyond that rank.

After a time, of course, the number of Hendon graduates was found to be heavily in excess of the vacancies available for Station Sub-Inspectors. A few of them did eventually become efficient Chief Constables in the provinces, but Hendon College, as such, did not survive, and I personally feel that it is not to be regretted. I am, of course, in no way deprecating the entry of university graduates into the police force—on the contrary. But I am convinced that a man who has a university degree does not *ipso facto* make a good policeman; and I am equally sure that there is no way of becoming a good senior police officer other than by starting at the bottom and spending at least a few years doing the work of an ordinary police constable. And here I would like to stress, also, that since many more ordinary constables are needed than senior officers, men who do not aspire to high positions but who are unwavering in their determination to discharge their simple duties conscientiously are no less necessary to the Force than are a smaller number of enterprising and ambitious men who work with rapid promotion in mind.

One other aspect of police life is often forgotten. I have emphasized how essential it is that the policeman himself should be the right type of man for the job. It is important also that his wife should be the right type of woman to be a policeman's wife. For although chances of promotion are good and there is a pension, newly-wedded wives tend to think less of the rather remote future than of the present. And many of them dislike very much that their husbands should be on duty occasionally on Saturdays and Sundays, and at night; they find it irksome that their private lives should be somewhat limited by their husbands' obligation to follow a rather straight and narrow path, and resent his insistence that they must remain a little choosey about their friends. And if a man's wife is not prepared to accept such limitations as her husband's duty imposes on them both, it is doubtful whether he will make good in his job.

Since nobody knew better than I how much was expected of the police, I was, as I have said, determined to see that my men received decent treatment in return. In this determination I was supported by Professor Webster. One of the first enthusiasms we shared was for the Sheffield section house (or residential barracks) for unmarried police officers. We found that the men had been living an unnecessarily frugal, uncared-for existence, cooking skimpy meals for themselves, cleaning their own rooms in off-duty hours, and looking after their clothes as best they could. I wanted these quarters to be a model establishment which we should feel proud to show to visitors. So I found a good matron to supervise the place and look after the men generally. I installed a cook who understood her job. And I had very little trouble in persuading my Watch Committee to spend some money on making the place comfortable and cheerful. Webster played his part by preparing diet sheets and giving his very assiduous attention to the health of the men in his care.

Some of my eminently practical schemes caused a certain amount of amusement, and among these was my introduction of a couple of steam-presses so that all police officers could leave their trousers to be pressed regularly, free of charge. The men are issued with two pairs of uniform trousers, so I felt they had now no excuse for ever looking other than smart and business-like, as they could always have one pair newly-pressed and ready to put on. I also arranged for wardrobe accommodation to be provided so that the officers could store in it either their winter or their summer uniform—whichever was not in use—for I had realized that in many of their little houses there was not adequate space for the proper hanging of this bulky clothing which frequently got crumpled and mishandled. There were great benefits derived from my solicitude for the men's clothes, apart from the improvement in their appearance, for the uniforms lasted nearly twice as long when they were properly looked after. Incidentally, I was able to provide useful work for two of our war-wounded officers, who were not fit for active service, but whom I sent to be trained to take charge of the presses, and who eventually performed this task most competently.

Another matter of police welfare which concerned both Webster and myself was the health of our veterans. One of the most depressing things that could happen to a policeman in those days was to fall sick or receive serious injury between his twenty-fifth and twenty-sixth year of service, for the rule was then that an officer could retire after twenty-five years' service on half-pay, but a pre-1919 entrant had only to serve for one more year to become entitled to a pension equal to two-thirds of his wages. It was most distressing to me to see how often a man who had weathered a quarter of a century would collapse and find himself invalided out on a medical certificate during the crucial twelve months which was to make so great a difference to his circumstances on his retirement.

Webster, would, therefore, give me a private report if he considered that a veteran officer was beginning to show signs of strain before his time for retirement was due, and my role was then to make sure he was transferred to a more sedentary job where he could continue to work efficiently until his twenty-six years were up. I found, for instance, that such men could be usefully employed in servicing and cleaning our fleet of Alvis cars, and generally they thoroughly enjoyed the change in their routine.

Another subject upon which Webster and I pondered together was the incidence of venereal disease among police officers. When one considers the number and variety of people with whom a police officer comes into contact, and the temptations he is exposed to, the percentage of men who contract V.D. is very small indeed—far smaller than that for other male civilians of corresponding ages and circumstances, and almost negligible when compared with the percentage for the fighting services. But there are a few victims.

To-day the cure, if taken in time, is almost alarmingly simple to effect, but in those days, if it were to be successful, treatment had to be received regularly over a long period. The man had two alternatives: he could go to an expensive and by no means reliable quack, and be haunted for the next fifteen to twenty years by the fear that this clandestine treatment had not been adequate and that he was doomed to succumb to general paralysis of the insane. Or he could attend the V.D. clinic at his own hospital—but if he chose this latter course he had to sit and wait his turn on a bench which was almost inevitably crowded with the scum of the town, to whom the policeman's guilty secret was thus revealed. This was not merely lowering to the prestige and morale of the Force, but was dangerous— for as I have pointed out already, there is always a risk that a policeman who gets into any sort of trouble will be black-mailed into protecting evil-doers in order to buy their silence.

Professor Webster put it to me, and I instantly agreed, that since occasional cases of V.D. among the police were inevit-able, it was far better to admit the fact and deal with it ade-quately. So we arranged that any police officer of any rank could go and explain his case to the Sheffield police surgeon and be treated for V.D. with no more comment than if he had reported sick with a cold. He need no longer go in fear of disgrace.

This attitude had, I am pleased to say, extremely good results —and there was no evidence that Sheffield's police officers exposed themselves more readily to the disease because we had made effective treatment easily available.

When I arrived in Sheffield, there were hardly any recrea-tional facilities for the police. They played occasional football or cricket matches, but always on pitches that were merely rented for a few shillings for the afternoon, and were often in very dingy and depressing neighbourhoods.

After much searching, we discovered a suitable ground and persuaded the Watch Committee and the Home Office to purchase it for us. This was the Niagara Ground at Wadsley Bridge and it made history in various ways, for not only did it become the first recreation ground ever to be acquired by a provincial police force exclusively for the use of its members, but it was also the ground on which the first British Police championships were held. It covered about ten acres, and was purchased from the late Dowager Duchess of Norfolk for £4,000.

The problems of adapting and equipping it for different sports, and of providing dressing-rooms with water, light, and sewerage, were solved by my staunch friend the City Treasurer, Mr. A. E. Griffiths, who persuaded the bank that carried the Police Recreation Society's account to permit an overdraft of £5,000 at a very low rate of interest, without any security except our word of honour. With our overdraft, a pavilion, dressing-rooms, baths, and tea-room and all necessary services were made possible. The pavilion, which was designed without fee by our good friend, Mr. W. G. Davies, the City Architect, was opened by H.R.H. The Princess Mary in August 1928.

We made a bowling green, five tennis courts, football, hockey, and cricket pitches, and a children's playground. £8,000 was spent on the ground in three years, and the extra £3,000 above the permitted overdraft was raised by the police themselves. At three of the stations, a regular programme of dances and whist drives helped to raise funds that were spent on the ground.

Though no one could be a more fervent advocate of police football than I, the Press were hugely delighted a little later on to be able to report that I had threatened to prohibit my men from playing the game on the grounds that it was too dangerous for them. I was also reported as considering hockey more suitable. I fear that for some little while the Sheffield police were mercilessly teased about this. The truth of the matter was that their enthusiasm for the game had on many occasions—especially in inter-divisional matches—led to rough-houses which were no integral part of a football match. I should not have complained, however, had it not been that as a result we had a stream of men suffering from injuries which prevented them from doing their work—though of course they continued to draw full pay. I could not countenance that, so I warned them that unless they could play football with reasonable regard for their arms and legs, I should be obliged to insist that they use Niagara for some gentler sport. Either the warning or the teasing which followed it produced the right results, however, and, in spite of their obligation to play less tempestuously, the Sheffield team won the local league cup not long afterwards and considered its honour vindicated.

My other preoccupations were with raising the morale of the men and with making them realize that they had a status in society which must not be degraded. For instance, it was quite usual in those days for householders to tip policemen if they had done anything to help them—particularly at Christmas—just as they tip postmen and dustmen. It seemed to me most unseemly for police officers to accept tips. I therefore made it an offence for any member of the Sheffield Force to accept one. Officers were instructed that if anyone insisted upon giving them money, they were to make it clear that it would be handed over to the Police Orphanage, and a receipt forwarded. I expected that this order might be unpopular, but, surprisingly, it was not. My men agreed that their dignity was worth more than a few shillings, and were glad to break away from a time-honoured but undesirable custom.

After seeing police boxes in Newcastle-upon-Tyne, I decided to introduce this admirable innovation to Sheffield. I must stress that the police box was not my own idea, as people sometimes seem to think, but that of Mr. F. J. Crawley, then Chief Constable of Newcastle-upon-Tyne. The great advantage is that a constable can go straight from his home to his beat, pick up the telephone, and report to his station that he has started work, signing a book provided for him in the box. When he finishes duty, he can go straight home after telephoning to report once more. This not only saves time, but prevents criminals from being able to count upon an almost certain lull in police patrols three times in every twenty-four hours, when, for about ten minutes, at 6 a.m., 2 p.m., and 10 p.m., all constables are busily making their way to or from the police station on their way on or off duty. The police box system means that they never know where an officer is likely to be.

It was not long after I had introduced the police box system to Sheffield that I had a visit from Superintendent (later Sir

George) Abbiss of the Metropolitan Police—who, incidentally, was later to become the first Assistant Commissioner of the Metropolitan Police to have risen from the ranks. It was after his inspection of the police boxes in Sheffield that they were introduced in London, where they are still used to-day.

Of course, this system means that one has to trust the constable to be as well turned out and in altogether as fit a state for duty as he would if he knew he had to put in a personal appearance at his station. But I have seldom found the police unworthy of trust, and in my experience good men work even better if they know they are trusted.

Another of my innovations designed to uphold the dignity of the police was one which—like the steam-presses—provoked much mirth at the outset. I arranged elocution classes for Sheffield constables. I had frequently been appalled at the mumbling incoherence of the men when they had to give evidence in court, and I was humiliated to see what sorry figures they often cut as a result of their inability to speak clearly when giving evidence. I therefore issued a notice, explaining that the classes were free and voluntary, and saying that I felt sure the men would welcome an opportunity of improving their speech. It was arranged that the training should teach them how to give evidence as well as correcting general faults. Much to everyone's surprise, the classes were very well attended and I do think an improvement was noticeable.

I have always been an advocate of women police, so it was a particular pleasure to me to do everything I could to encourage and assist the three valiant pioneers who had already been sworn in as constables in Sheffield when I arrived there. They were Mary Winn, Mary Morris, and Barbara Watson, and they were doing street and park patrols in uniform, escorting women prisoners to Manchester Prison, and performing court duties. They were also employed on plain clothes work with the C.I.D. There was some prejudice against them, but they were remarkably intelligent and courageous women and soon convinced most people that they were willing to take the rough work in their stride; and it could be very rough indeed for them sometimes, for they inevitably had a large share of unpleasant jobs. By 1928, the strength of women police was increased to one sergeant and five constables, and to-day there are two sergeants and fourteen constables. And a splendid job they do! One of Sheffield's policewomen in my day, incidentally, was Barbara Denis de Vitré, who is now an Assistant Inspector of Constabulary at the Home Office, and the first woman ever to be offered an appointment of that nature.

CHAPTER TEN

A famous test case – The end of newspaper football pools.

I HAVE never had a cheque in my morning mail signed by Messrs. Littlewood, Vernon, or Cope. Yet I cannot help feeling that they owe me a debt of gratitude for I am the man who—indirectly—gave them their start in life—and they have done fairly well as a result, if a few millions are any measure of success.

It is difficult for many of us to remember, and for the younger ones to believe, that until 1928 all football pools in Britain were run by newspapers and Mr. Littlewood had not been heard of at all. The usual method of the newspapers was to print a list of twenty to forty-four matches, and invite readers to forecast the results of twelve to twenty-four of these games, which were to be played on the next Saturday. The prizes were always cash, varying from £200 in the smaller newspapers, to as much as £30,000 in the national Sunday papers.

The advantage to the newspapers offering these large sums of money was that few readers contented themselves with buying merely one copy of the paper in question, but would purchase two or three dozen copies each to obtain the special forecast coupons, in the hope that their chances of winning would be thus increased.

Actually their mathematical chances have been calculated fairly accurately. To forecast twenty-four matches out of forty-four, it would be necessary to send in 282,429,526,481 differing coupons before one could be sure of giving all correct results. These odds, you may think, are not to be greatly reduced by purchasing a mere dozen extra copies. Fortunately for the newspapers concerned, the average man did not appear at the time to realize this, and permutations were as unknown as Littlewood.

In 1927 the situation was such that a newspaper was almost forced to run a football pool contest in order to survive. If it did not, its circulation figures would show up very badly against those of its competitors, even though nine out of every ten of their copies sold were thrown away unread as soon as the coupon had been clipped from them. Yet these newspaper football pools were so much an accepted part of our daily lives that very few of us gave a second thought to them.

My own views upon football pools in newspapers were practically non-existent, except for a vague uneasiness in my conscience whenever some publican or shopkeeper had to be prosecuted for having "fruit machines" on the premises; or some bookie's "runner" was fined for street betting; I felt that this was all somewhat unfair upon the "little man" as long as the big organizer was left free to organize newspaper football pools. Then one day I read a comment in some law periodical, by a judge of the high court—or it may have been the Attorney-General—that he did not understand why police action had never been taken against the newspaper football pools, on the grounds that they were illegal, being a lottery.

In Sheffield at this time we had a very famous magistrates' clerk, Mr. F. B. Dingle, who was for many years the editor of *Stone's Justices' Manual*—the handbook of all Justices of the Peace who take their places upon the benches of magistrates' courts. Mr. Dingle, known affectionately as "Pa" Dingle, was a lovable and forthright man. I went and talked to him about the law as it seemed to relate to newspaper football pools. I had to remember that "Pa" Dingle would have the task of advising the Sheffield magistrates upon points of law, in any action I might bring, and was not, therefore, in a position to permit himself to advise me beforehand on the line I should take. He was, however, able to elucidate for me one or two points of law, and after our talk I decided that I was justified in going ahead.

I am aware that to many people it seemed that I went out of my way for no very good reason to stir up a great deal of trouble; and that it was suspected some personal grudge or quirk of character had provoked me to take action. For me, however, the situation was plain and quite simple. It had been suggested that newspaper football pools were illegal. I was not sure if this was so, but, as a man responsible for enforcing the law of this country, it was my duty to find out. If it were so, then it was my duty to prevent such infringement of the law. The moral issue did not enter into the problem; nor did any personal feeling of approval or disapproval I might have had of betting or football pools. If a law is unjust, or susceptible of misinterpretation—why then, it should be changed! But not merely by tacit agreement because large interests are involved, nor because it is commonly supposed by people in the public eye that it is imprudent to rub the Press up the wrong way. And not, in any case, I think, at the discretion of a Chief Constable.

I have sometimes been asked why I did not leave action to be taken by a larger police force against a national newspaper. The only answer I can give is that there had been plenty of time for action to have been taken against a national newspaper, and so far the challenge to the police—for so I considered it to be—had remained unanswered. It was no business of mine what happened elsewhere, but what happened in Sheffield *was* my business—and if there was a wrong there I should put right, I did not consider that I could excuse myself from doing so by reflecting that there were bigger wrongs elsewhere which no one was bothering about.

In Sheffield, the eminently respectable *Sheffield Daily Telegraph* was running a flourishing football pool contest, with prizes each week of £1,000 for twenty-four all-correct results or £200 for the nearest. The contest cost the paper about £8,000 a year to run. The coupons were posted in collection-boxes that were sited not only in the front office of the newspaper, but in other parts of Sheffield, and I was able to discover that from a single box 17,000 envelopes (each containing presumably at least one coupon) were collected at a time. Obviously, the *Sheffield Daily Telegraph* had a greatly enhanced "false" circulation apart from those copies sold to be read. Thousands of people must be buying copies merely for the football pools.

Yet it might be argued that this was not a lottery. There had to be a certain skill in choosing the teams most likely to win. But, though one could not discount this, I still did not feel satisfied and, in July 1927, I told Sir Charles Clifford, the proprietor of the *Sheffield Daily Telegraph*, that I proposed to prosecute his newspaper. I informed him of my intention in the friendliest possible manner, emphasizing that I was regarding the matter as a test case to establish whether or not football forecast competitions were legal, and that no criticism of the *Sheffield Daily Telegraph*, specifically, was implied.

He was amused at first, and took it in very good part. He set his legal advisers to work, and the result was that within a fortnight the competition was reorganized: nobody might send in more than thirteen coupons, of which six were to be taken from the morning newspapers, six from the evening papers and one from the Saturday football extra. The idea of this was to make a defence against any accusation that the paper was being purchased solely for its football pool coupon. This way, it seemed, the proprietors of the *Sheffield Daily Telegraph* could claim that each copy was purchased upon its own merits, and that the pools coupon was incidental.

It was undeniably ingenious. But still I was not satisfied. When I told Sir Charles Clifford that I still proposed to prosecute his firm (Sir W. C. Long & Co., Ltd.), as proprietors of the *Sheffield Daily Telegraph* for contravening the 1920 Ready-Money Football Betting Act, by publishing a football competition coupon, he was obviously amused no longer.

As from my point of view it was simply a test case, when it came up in the magistrates' court I asked for only a nominal fine. But the attitude of the *Sheffield Daily Telegraph*, from the moment the summons was served, changed.

Eventually in July 1928, the *Sheffield Daily Telegraph* was summoned at Sheffield Magistrates' Court for having published on March 9 a coupon of a ready-money football betting business contrary to the Ready-Money Football Betting Act, 1920, and for publishing an advertisement about this.

The Ready-Money Football Betting Act was intended specifically to stop bookmakers from sending coupons out by thousands, particularly to factories. When it was introduced by Colonel Sir Henry Norris, he had said: "The Bill does not in any way stop anyone from having a bet on the result of a particular match. Nor does it attempt to stop the competitions which one sees advertised by various periodicals for a prize for which there is no entrance fee." My own belief was, however, that the newspapers were breaking the law, even though the man who introduced the law had taken the trouble to explain that it was not aimed at restraining them. I was generously advised on all sides that I stood an excellent chance of making an abject fool of myself.

The case for the police was put to the Magistrates carefully by Mr. Paley Scott. People were being invited, he said, either skilfully to estimate or luckily to guess which team would win in each of the matches set out on the coupon, and the person who most nearly obtained the correct results received £200. An important alteration had been made in the rules of the competition. Prior to August 8, any competitor could send in as many coupons as he liked. This meant that a man, speculating his money on buying, say, a dozen copies of the newspaper, was buying at least eleven for the sole purpose of obtaining the coupons and increasing his chances of winning.

This, it was submitted by the police, would be betting and nothing else. But, even after the newspaper made its new rule that limited the number of coupons that could be sent in, we contended that it was still betting. "The Prosecution brings this case in no vindictive spirit," said Mr. Paley Scott, "but because the authorities desire to know whether these competitions are an infringement of the law."

The Defence submitted that the newspapers were merely promoting the interests of their readers in football, and that the competition had nothing to do with gambling, betting, or wagering. The Bench, said Mr. Cassels, K.C., who appeared for the *Sheffield Daily Telegraph*, must distinguish between the sporting sheet issued solely for the purpose of attracting money through the coupon, and the honest, straightforward general newspaper, such as the *Sheffield Daily Telegraph*.

The Bench (Mr. Walter Appleyard and Mrs. Winifred

Williams) decided to convict, with a fine of £5, on the grounds that they had concluded "these newspapers are bought very largely and extensively for the sake of the coupons alone". They felt that the case should go before a higher tribunal, being of national importance.

The Magistrates stated a case for an appeal, and on 22nd November 1928, at a King's Bench Divisional Court, Lord Hewart, the Lord Chief Justice, Mr. Justice Acton, and Mr. Justice Avory heard it. Mr. Stuart Bevan, K.C., Mr. J. D. Cassels, K.C., and Mr. Theobold Matthew appeared for the *Sheffield Daily Telegraph*. We opposed them with Mr. R. M. Montgomery, K.C., and Mr. Paley Scott.

The main point at issue was whether, when a person paid a penny to buy the *Sheffield Daily Telegraph*, any part of that penny was paid for the coupon. If it was, then this was betting. The Defence insisted that the penny was for the newspaper, and that the coupon was merely incidental.

Mr. Bevan said that the newspaper's point of view was that, by reason of running the competition, it was bringing the newspaper with all its advantages to the notice of persons who might otherwise have overlooked it. This was, he said, very different. The same newspaper, he explained, gave free insurance policies, a crossword puzzle, and the Stock Exchange prices. Could a newspaper be said to be carrying on an insurance business? And in the same way, should it be argued that it was carrying on a betting business?

Asked to define what was and what was not a betting business, Mr. Bevan suggested the example of a bookseller who had a circulating library, and held it as one of the terms that in taking out their monthly subscription, library members should enter into a free competition as to the most popular book of the year. A prize would be offered and no increase made in the subscription. This, submitted Mr. Bevan, would not be a betting business, as it was merely incidental to the bookselling business.

Mr. Justice Avory asked: "If an old-established greengrocer set up a betting business and made it a condition that he would not make a bet with anyone unless they bought a carrot from

him, would that business come within the Act in question?"
His own opinion was that it was a case where a man who wanted
to make a bet had to buy a carrot even if he didn't want one!

The appeal was dismissed with costs, and the same evening
all London newspapers announced that they had decided to
stop football competitions forthwith.

At the same time, the Incorporated Society of British Advertisers Limited—the most influential organization of its kind in
the country—unanimously passed a resolution declaring that
circulations obtained by coupon competitions "represent false
values in number and quality, and that such competitions
lower not only the tone and the dignity of the newspapers
running them, but the influence and prestige of the newspapers, and, as a consequence, of advertisers' names associated
with them". It was certainly true, as Lord Hewart had pointed
out during the appeal, that if a man bought the millions of
copies necessary to make sure of winning the prize, the circulation went up by so much, and the advertising charges went
up accordingly, even if the purchaser did not read one of the
newspapers, but simply cut out the coupons.

That day saw the death of football coupons in newspapers in
Britain. It opened the way for the present-day system, of
course, but this—whatever its other advantages or disadvantages—is at least legal. And it leaves the newspapers free to
get on with their own more serious business.

For me, I repeat, the affair was just another plain police job
and my course of action was not taken for any other reason
than to ascertain what precisely was the law, and, having done
this, to ensure that it was enforced. While the case was in
progress, however, many people in Sheffield felt very bitterly
towards me. I remember that a Conservative M.P. for one of
the Sheffield Divisions lost his seat and blamed me roundly,
though why, precisely, I never discovered.

My own most vivid memory of the local repercussions is of
one night when, after returning from London with Detective-
Inspector George Manifold, I called in at the White Horse
Hotel at Eaton Socon for a drink with him. To my surprise,
everybody in the bar was loudly and heatedly discussing this

football pools business. Everybody—understandably, I suppose—seemed to be very much opposed to the prosecution. The main theme of the discussion was that this terrible new Chief Constable of Sheffield, who had come in from nowhere, seemed set upon making trouble.

The landlady, a very charming woman, was holding forth against this fellow Sillitoe. Naturally, I joined in, agreeing with her heartily, and George Manifold, grinning widely, did the same.

Mrs. Chantry and everybody in the bar warmed to us at once. "And what business are you gentlemen in?" asked Mrs. Chantry. "Are you in the steel business?"

"No," I said, "we're in the anti-steal business. I am this terrible new Chief Constable of Sheffield we have been discussing."

They were very nice about it.

CHAPTER ELEVEN

The murder of P.C. Gutteridge – I set in train a routine investigation of a minor offence that leads to the killers.

I HAVE met and dealt with killers. Some escaped with a verdict of culpable homicide, and others were hanged. Two among them joined the most notorious in the Chamber of Horrors, and I want to tell their story because it seems to me to shed a very significant light on police work. This, a most brutal and baffling murder case, was finally solved not by any brilliant individual detective work, but by the police of a suburban district of Sheffield, who, without thinking of glory, glamour, or headlines—or even of murder—were just doing their duty, following a simple, tedious police routine, knocking on doors, asking questions, checking car numbers. In search of a minor traffic offender they were making patient progress —when, suddenly, they found instead a murderer.

Credit for the solving of the notorious Browne and Kennedy case—the murder of P.C. Gutteridge—went to Scotland Yard. I think it is only fair to say that it was due to "F" Division of Sheffield City Police.

When the body of P.C. Gutteridge was discovered in a quiet country lane, everyone was appalled and revolted to learn that he had been shot through each eye as he lay dying. P.C. Gutteridge was not one of my policemen. He had belonged to the Essex County Constabulary for seventeen years. Yet I felt close to him, perhaps because he seemed to be so typically the village policeman. One could imagine him in shirt-sleeves on his afternoons off, digging his bit of garden next to the cottage that was also the police station, with no more to give it authority than a notice, a telephone, and a pair of spare handcuffs in a drawer of the kitchen sideboard, kept there along with his wife's weekly insurance book and the best Sunday table cloth.

He would have finished his supper tea, carefully knocked out his pipe against the fireplace, and said: "See you later, dear," to his wife in the kitchen, before he opened the cottage door to begin his routine night patrol of the quiet lanes that he knew so well.

When the body of P.C. Gutteridge was found next day, his helmet lay on the ground beside him. His notebook was also dropped on the road. His carefully-sharpened bit of pencil was clutched tightly in his stiff fingers. There was no sign of a struggle. His truncheon was undisturbed in his trousers pocket. His lantern had been switched off and returned to his belt. Whatever he had intended to write, he must have been standing in a light that somebody else had provided—presumably car headlamps. Car-tyre marks supported this theory.

There was a car reported stolen that night from Dr. Lovell's garage, twelve miles away. The same morning that P.C. Gutteridge was discovered murdered, Dr. Lovell's car was found abandoned in Brixton. There were human bloodstains on the running-board and a recently-fired empty cartridge case on the floorboards. In calibre it was the same as the bullet that killed P.C. Gutteridge.

This car was taken to the country lane where the murder had been done, and its tyre-marks fitted exactly those which the Essex police were carefully preserving at the murder site. It was obvious that if the occupants of that stolen car could be found, the authorities would have gone a long way towards finding the killer of P.C. Gutteridge.

At this time, in my police headquarters at Sheffield—quite a distance from the scene—I had recently devised a new bit of red tape. I did not know then that this red tape would eventually ensnare the murderers. The circumstances were that I had been perturbed by some lack of uniformity in my police divisions over minor traffic offences. One divisional superintendent would prosecute where another would caution for the same type of offence. I felt that this needed central control, and had special forms printed, upon which all details of motoring offences were to be entered, and I—as Chief Constable—would decide what should be done in each case.

The murder of P.C. Gutteridge had taken place in Essex. Nearly three months passed. The case did not touch our boundaries, and we maintained only the same sympathetic, watchful interest, with which all England was following the unfruitful hunt. Neither the Essex police nor bearded Inspector Berrett of Scotland Yard, who was in charge of the inquiries, had managed to get any further.

What had happened, of course, was that Browne and Kennedy had left London by train to go to Billericay and steal a car that was in a private garage there. Browne, who was an expert motor mechanic, had a garage in Clapham, and Kennedy worked for him. Both were ex-convicts, and they had met in gaol. They worked in the daytime doing normal garage repair jobs, and at night made excursions out into the countryside to steal cars, which they disguised or stripped of spare parts. Browne had developed a technique of buying scrap-heap cars and exhibiting them to clients with the promise that he would "do them up until they looked almost brand-new". A week or two afterward he would deliver a car of the same make in excellent condition—he or his accomplice had stolen it, and false registration number-plates, faked engine-numbers, and disguised paint work perfected its resemblance to the scrap-heap car.

He had done several ingenious insurance frauds. He fixed a telephone so that when it rang a fire would start in his garage. He went to Bournemouth, made an alibi for himself, then calmly phoned his garage and set it ablaze.

He served a term of imprisonment in Parkhurst Prison and was sent to Dartmoor for four years' penal servitude on further offences after that. He did every day of his sentence, deliberately sacrificing good-conduct remission, so that when he had finished his time he would not be under police supervision as a "ticket-of-leave man".

During his last few days in Dartmoor he said to the Governor: "When I leave this place I'll 'crack' your house!" He carried out his threat, apparently, for within twenty-four hours of his release from Dartmoor the Governor's house was in fact burgled and all his most precious household treasures either stolen or smashed. But Browne had an alibi that the police could not break.

Browne was a vicious man, feared among his criminal associates. Kennedy, on the other hand, was always hungry for popularity and if he could get it no other way would buy it in public houses by flashing his money. He had had a good education. He was a grammar-school boy, and became a compositor in Liverpool. His first offence was for indecency, and for this he lost not only his job but his reputation. After that he plunged into crime—not perhaps inspired by the same incentives of greed and self-aggrandisement as Browne—but with equally wholehearted enthusiasm. Both men, in their different ways, had decided that they had a war to wage against society.

Typical, I think, of Kennedy's nature was his behaviour after the murder hunt had grown to its climax, when Browne had been arrested and Kennedy was in fact "on the run", knowing the police wanted him. He had just got married and was staying on his honeymoon in West Kirby. Here, though he was a gaol-bird and was well aware that he had been an accomplice in a horrible murder, and though he slept each night with a loaded revolver beside his lodging-house bed, he did not think it prudent to avoid behaviour that would draw attention to himself. In the nearby public house he ostentatiously bought drinks for strangers, seeking to impress them by flashing five-pound notes—which were by no means common in those days in West Kirby pubs.

Such, then, were Browne and Kennedy. Both men had a smouldering hatred of the police, the human obstacles between them and the fulfilment of their ambitions.

On the night of P.C. Gutteridge's murder, they set out on a trip to Billericay, to steal a car that they knew to be in a garage there. They took a train to Billericay, intending to drive back to London in the stolen car whilst its owner slept peacefully, believing it to be safe in the garage.

But no sooner had the two thieves got to the garage than a dog began to bark. Kennedy wanted to return to London empty-handed. Had they done so, both might have escaped hanging. But Browne was stronger-minded. He hated to admit failure. Perhaps he hated to seem afraid. At any rate, he insisted upon looking for another garage that could be broken open.

Their eventual victim was Dr. Lovell in the same village of Billericay, and from this garage they took a Morris-Cowley. It was in this stolen car that Browne and Kennedy were returning at high speed to their Clapham workshop when P.C. Gutteridge waved to them to stop and blew his whistle.

The constable could hardly have known that the car was stolen, for it had not yet been missed by Dr. Lovell. It is just possible that Gutteridge recognized it, but the greater probability is that it was being driven recklessly. Browne was a supremely competent handler of cars, but he was also entirely inconsiderate of anybody else's safety.

He was driving upon a rural side-track that he had chosen precisely because it kept well away from the main thoroughfare. When the policeman signalled him, Browne stopped. He expected, no doubt, to bluff his way past a sleepy village constable. Gutteridge asked Browne if he had a driving licence. According to Kennedy, Browne stammered in his answer and when the policeman inquired if the car was his, Kennedy interrupted, saying it belonged to him. When the policeman asked Browne if he knew the number, Browne told him that he would see it on the front of the car. Gutteridge replied that *he* knew the number, but did Browne? Eventually Kennedy gave the number—TW 6180. Gutteridge, his suspicions aroused by the rather odd replies he had received from Browne, apparently decided to take particulars. As he pulled his notebook from his pocket, about to write in it, Browne fired at him. The bullet entered the constable's cheekbone, and he reeled across the road to the opposite bank. It is not clear what happened afterwards. Browne declared to the judge that Kennedy fired the two shots into P.C. Gutteridge's dying eyes. Kennedy declared in court that these two shots—among the most vicious in all British criminal history—were aimed by Browne.

For what it is worth, I am inclined to feel that Kennedy's

story may be the more credible. He told the court at his trial that after Browne fired the first shot he got out of the car and went after the wounded constable. Kennedy declared that he pleaded with Browne and said, "For God's sake, don't shoot any more, the man's dying."

But Browne had apparently seen some nightmarish accusation in the police officer's eyes, for he muttered: "What are you looking at me like that for?" and carefully put a bullet in each of P.C. Gutteridge's eyes. There was a suggestion at his trial that Browne might have been a believer in the superstition that the eyes of a dying man photograph the last thing he sees.

The two murderers drove on and later abandoned the car. Next day, Browne was working unconcernedly in his garage, and Kennedy, although grievously troubled, was still in control of himself. There was, at that time, no workable clue to link them with the murder.

Scotland Yard were called in and Chief Detective-Inspector Berrett was assigned to the case. But, though exhaustive inquiries were made by both the Yard and the Essex Police, after six weeks the murderer had not been identified.

Then, on 14th November 1927, a van driver named John Mincher complained to Constable 395 James William Ward of "F" Division of the Sheffield City Police that he had been driving quite slowly down Douglas Road, and was passing through a railway arch, when a motor-car with number plates XK 2508 came speeding towards him, plunged at the bridge which was not wide enough for both vehicles, and forced the van-driver to swerve against the wall of the railway arch.

Mincher's mudguard was damaged. The car stopped for a moment and Mincher asked for the driver's name and address, but was refused it. The car then drove away and Mincher complained to the police.

Police-Constable Ward kept a careful look out and not long after saw a Vauxhall car with the number XK 2508 in Penistone Road. He spoke to the driver and asked to see his driving licence.

There were two men in the car. The driver showed his

licence, and P.C. Ward copied down the name and address: "Sydney Rhodes, 27 York Terrace, Clapham Road, Stockwell, S.W."

All these details came to me on a "Traffic Offence Form", and I decided that the driver should be prosecuted for dangerous driving. I sent the name and address to the Metropolitan Police, and requested that the driver of the car be located so that a summons might be served upon him. After ten days, the Metropolitan Police reported back to me that the number was that of a London taxi, which was a Beardmore and not a Vauxhall, and that the driver could not be traced at the address I had given. I sent the papers back to them and insisted that the guilty driver and the car be found. Again the papers were returned to me without result. I realized that I had asked for a great deal. So far as the Yard were concerned, this was quite a simple traffic offence. Nobody had been injured and they did not feel disposed to make a major hue-and-cry of it.

I sent for the Superintendent of Walkley Division and said: "The Yard say they can't find this man, so we must do it ourselves. We'll comb Attercliffe for a start, to see if he called on anyone there. A hooligan like this deserves to be prosecuted!"

The Superintendent ordered a door-to-door inquiry to be made through Attercliffe, and this went on for nearly a month. Attercliffe was being carefully and exhaustively turned inside out, for we were seeking anybody who could tell us anything about the Vauxhall car with the false number-plates.

Now this may not sound the most exciting part of the story, but to my mind it is by far the most interesting: that the police of an entire division should pursue such a relatively trivial inquiry with such zealous persistence that the one man in Attercliffe who knew the identity of that car driver began to lose his nerve.

For Supt. Plant of this Division not only kept his men to the search, but also kept changing P.C. Ward's beat, so that the only officer who had seen the car and its two occupants might have every chance of glimpsing somewhere upon the street, in shop, house, or pub, either of the two men he had seen in the car.

Eventually, Constable Ward did see a man whose face seemed like that of the passenger in the wanted car—which was wanted, remember, not in connection with murder, but merely for denting a van's mudguard. Constable Ward re-reported this to his superiors, and it was discovered that the man was named Charles Rhodes Currie, a butcher who lived in Douglas Terrace, Sheffield.

"But I know that man," said Supt. Plant. "He's got a criminal record. I put him away myself, nearly twenty years ago."

P.C. Ward was put to watch Currie's butcher shop in Burgoyne Road, in the hope that the car driver might again turn up to visit the butcher. Meanwhile, Supt. Plant himself had a word with Currie, and tried to persuade him to say who the driver was.

At first, Currie denied all knowledge of the incident, and was perfectly safe in doing so, for there was no evidence against him, nor had he committed any offence. But the search and the inquiries were kept up, and one day my chief clerk came in to say that there was a man named Currie at the Inquiry Office counter who wanted to see me personally and alone.

This was significant, for it was apparent to anybody who understood police routine that an ordinary man-in-the-street who wished to see the Chief Constable would have found himself being sympathetically interviewed by an officer of the Criminal Investigation Department, or a Court Missionary, before he got to the Chief Constable's office. It seemed, there-fore, that this man Currie knew his way about the police administration, for he had stubbornly resisted all suggestions that he should talk to a C.I.D. officer.

I buzzed to my C.I.D.: "Do you know anything about a chap named Currie?" "Yes, sir—an ex-convict, keeps a butcher's shop in Attercliffe, several previous convictions."

With this information I told my chief clerk to send Currie in to me. I was quite willing to see him alone, if that was how he wanted it. Currie came in, his hands twitching nervously. He sat down and we discussed a few generalities. There was a long, painful silence, then Currie suddenly blurted out: "I know why you're so hot on these Attercliffe inquiries, sir—and I want you to understand that I had nothing to do with the murder!"

This came right out of the blue to me. I said carefully: "Naturally, with your kind of record, Currie, you don't want to be mixed up in anything you are not responsible for, particularly murder."

Currie said quickly: "I wasn't in the car—I wasn't with Browne and Kennedy when they shot him. I didn't even know they were on that job."

"You didn't?"

"No, sir—Browne came up to Attercliffe afterwards to ask me if I'd take the revolver he used on Gutteridge—he said if the police jumped him for anything he didn't want to have it on him."

"It was a remarkably long way to come, don't you think?" I said, keeping my voice as non-committal as I could. Currie hesitated, then said: "Well, sir—I can see you know about it—he did ask me to come in on this other job. 'There's a chap coming out of the Moor in a fortnight, Charlie,' he said, 'and we can do a four-handed job.' But honestly, Mr. Sillitoe, I told him I wanted nothing to do with it and I wouldn't take that gun off him, though he threatened me."

"I see," I said. Currie was sitting right on the edge of his chair, and his face was harrowed with anxiety. "If Browne ever gets to think I grassed (informed) on him, sir," he said, "he'll shoot me, too!"

I need hardly say that as soon as my office door had closed behind Currie, I sprang to action more quickly than ever I had in my life before. Within a few seconds I was on the phone to Scotland Yard.

Eventually we found that Browne had stolen the Vauxhall from somewhere near Birmingham, and, finding himself not far from the home of his criminal acquaintance, Currie, decided to drive to Attercliffe and have a talk with him.

Browne was known to be a car thief and to carry a gun—facts which corroborated Currie's story. Five Scotland Yard officers went to his garage in Clapham, and waited for him. They knew the type of man he was. When he drove into his garage, got out of his car, and strolled unsuspectingly into his little office to find himself surrounded by policemen, he smiled cynically. "If you had stopped me in the car, I should have shot five of you and saved the sixth for myself," he said, and added thoughtfully: "I shall have to get a machine gun for you bastards next time!"

This remark indicates the mental processes of criminals who shoot policemen. But for Browne there was no next time.

He had two loaded Webley revolvers in his car, and a third pistol hanging from a hook over his bed. Yet another loaded gun was hidden in an out-house lavatory, and almost as soon as Browne had been arrested he asked permission to use this lavatory. The police sensibly searched it first and found the gun.

Kennedy, who was still on his honeymoon in Liverpool when the police came for him, ran out of his lodgings into the street with a raincoat thrown over his undervest and trousers. When Det.-Sergt. Mathieson of the Liverpool City Police closed on him he produced his revolver and pulled the trigger. But, in his anxiety to kill the police officer, he forgot about the safety-catch, or else he jammed the cocking-hammer against the flesh of his hand, for the gun misfired. He was not given time for a second attempt.

When the police had the gun, and after they had taken photomicrographs of the way the barrel-riflings marked each bullet it fired, and compared them with the bullets found in Gutteridge's body, the case for the Prosecution was complete.

This was, I believe, the first case in English law in which it was accepted that a gun always leaves its "fingerprint"—its own particular pattern of scratches and markings—upon each bullet it fires, so that police scientists can always tell if a given bullet was fired from a certain weapon. Browne and Kennedy were no friends of the police. But they were instrumental in establishing a legal precedent that has since helped to hang many gunmen.

From his prison cell, Browne, using his urine as invisible ink, wrote a message to Currie on the back of a letter from his wife to Mabel Currie, a child of eleven. The message read: "Can you tell the date when Pat Kennedy divided a small heap of jewellery in two, and I tossed up to see which I should take (he the other). Will you let me know by return the date it was that I exchanged revolvers with Kennedy after he may have shot P.C. Just quote date as near as possible. Fred." Since the evidence seems to prove fairly conclusively that it was Browne who fired the fatal shots, it seems probable that he wrote this message in the belief that it would be intercepted— as indeed it was. However that may be, both men were convicted of murder, and both were hanged.

I had one further link with the Browne and Kennedy case. The *News of the World* had offered a reward of £2,000 for information leading to the conviction of the murderer. Logically, Currie the butcher was the man to receive this reward, and I took steps to see that he got it.

CHAPTER TWELVE

I become Chief Constable of Glasgow – Clearing the way for promotion and reorganizing the police divisions – The police box system instituted – My visit to the United States and the introduction of radio cars for the Glasgow flying squad.

THE post of Chief Constable to the city of Glasgow—"the second city", as many Scots proudly call it—is an important one. The police force there was second in strength to that of the Metropolitan Force of London. When the post became vacant in 1931, candidates applied from all over the Commonwealth, for it was a plum of the profession with a salary of £1,500 rising to £2,000.

The Glasgow Police Committee finally chose me to fill the vacancy, largely, I think, because at that time the city was overrun by gangsters terrorizing other citizens and waging open war between themselves in the streets, and I, with my experience of Sheffield, was thought to be capable of dealing with them.

I was soon to be made aware, however, that my appointment was not universally popular in Glasgow. There were a number of newspaper articles questioning the wisdom of "going across the Border to find a Chief Constable". Shortly after my arrival, the Glasgow Police held their annual concert at St. Andrews Hall, and the chairman, Sir John Cargill, stressed in his speech that it was a great privilege to be a Scotsman. He had, he said, a varied knowledge of the world and a fair knowledge of people of different nationalities, and he was absolutely certain that the Scottish people were the finest in the world and that Scotland was the most beautiful country. Then he added: "We have with us to-night the new Chief Constable, Captain Sillitoe. I am sure that Glasgow will give him the open-handed welcome which it always accords to strangers. It is an old saying that a new broom sweeps clean, and no doubt Captain Sillitoe has brought the new broom with him in his kitbag from Sheffield. But probably no one knows better than Sillitoe that he has not come here to be the head of the Cleansing Department, and I am sure he will find there are neither flies nor cobwebs upon the Glasgow Police!"

There were cheers at this. Unfortunately I had not been long in my new job before I began to discover that there were large swarms of flies on the police administration. The cobwebs were to be found on the promotion system. There was a great deal that needed most urgently to be done by the police: there were the gangsters and a lot of petty crime besides; there were trouble-making Communists; and, as I was soon to suspect, there was graft and corruption in the Corporation. It was essential, therefore, that my new broom should be brought into immediate operation, no matter how disturbing the spring-cleaning might be, for without an efficient and contented police force under me I could do nothing in any of these matters.

When I went to Glasgow the average constable could not hope ever to be more than a "puller of padlocks", doomed to spend thirty years or so "shaking hands with doorknobs". This was due in some measure to the fact that most of the senior officers were men of very ripe age who had been promoted years ago and had remained in their positions. Now, in my opinion, a job where there is no chance of promotion is not calculated to bring out the best in a young man. Also, it is my conviction that almost anyone can stay too long in a job; police work, particularly, needs new, fresh ideas, and active energy not to be found in men who have stayed put for most of their lives and grown old performing the same routines day after day. I therefore took upon myself the task—which was painful to me, too—of reminding nearly all my senior officers that they had qualified for pensions long ago or, in some cases, were just about to do so, and that I expected them to retire. Naturally, this came as a blow to some of them, and a few received my intimation with very bad grace. One who had been a superintendent since 1908, declared himself "grossly insulted", and wrote to the newspapers to announce this. However, I called a voluntary meeting of the police and informed the 1,500 men who came that I was trying to clear the way for promotion—strictly on merit, of course—and I explained my policy in regard to senior officers: that, in the interests of efficiency, retirement would be compulsory as soon as they became entitled to their maximum pensions. A roar of approval came from my constables. At the same time, I told the men that I hoped to inaugurate a system of police boxes, and explained the advantages they would give. I also invited all ranks from Inspector downwards to enter a competition with a prize of five guineas for submitting a plan to reorganize the city's police divisions so as to reduce wastage of men and administrative labour.

I left the City Hall after that meeting convinced that I had the great majority of the city's police officers on my side. I immediately sent two of my senior officers to Sheffield to study the police box system I had introduced there; I also seized the opportunity to bring to Glasgow two of my best Sheffield sergeants—one a specialist in mechanized transport, and the other, Sergeant Hammond, my fingerprint and photo-micrography expert.

My eventual reorganization of the police divisions, reducing them from eleven to seven, made an economy of £28,000 a year for Glasgow. I felt justified therefore in asking that some of this amount be spent on police boxes, patrol cars, and scientific equipment.

The first scheme was to erect 323 police boxes and ten telephone pillars at strategic points throughout the city. Each box would be a miniature police station, equipped with a telephone loudspeaker behind a grille into which a person could talk directly with Divisional Police Headquarters. There was, besides, a small office where the constable on duty could sit and write out his reports, conduct interviews, and so on; and could, moreover, eat his sandwiches without having to beg shelter from householders or café proprietors along his beat. At some, there was even a cell for detaining persons until they could be picked up in transport from headquarters.

I tried to make it clear that the sale of police buildings which, as a result, would become redundant, could be expected to produce £121,000 for the city treasury, while the cost of my police box scheme could be met for £36,000. But, although the Police Committee approved the scheme in theory, it required that it should be spread over five years. However, by 1938 we had all the boxes working and were getting useful calls from ordinary citizens—reporting any untoward incidents—at the rate of about sixty a week. The first aid cabinets that were built into the boxes also came in useful and were brought into service over one thousand times in 1938. Primarily, though, as I explained earlier, the advantage was that my constables did not waste time reporting to headquarters and could remain on their beats until they were actually relieved.

The next step was to arrange that the police were able to get to any place where there was trouble as quickly as possible. I started a mobile squad of police cars, but it was the United States which offered an excellent example in solving the problem of communication. In 1933 I went to Chicago to attend a convention of the International Association of Chiefs of Police. It was then that I met Mr. J. Edgar Hoover for the first time. Though I could not be sure beforehand how great a benefit I should derive from this trip, I did feel there might be something I could learn. This was the only defence I could put up to certain members of the Corporation who accused me—rather churlishly, I thought—of going "just for the joy-ride". Anyway, in the course of my three weeks' stay in America I managed to inspect not only the Chicago police system, but also those of New York, Los Angeles, Berkeley, and Portland, Oregon.

In 1932 the New York Police Force had begun to pioneer the use of radio patrol cars. I had read about this, and was most anxious to see it. I had already approached various prominent radio manufacturers in England, and had been told that it was utterly impossible and impracticable to build a two-way radio that would be light enough for an ordinary police patrol car to carry. It is strange now to think that this was less than twenty years ago.

But in New York I actually saw the type of radio that I wanted, fitted into a police car and transmitting and receiving messages in Morse or speech. This was exactly the sort of instrument that I had been told by English manufacturers it was "madness to hope to get".

I felt sure that it was only a question of time—perhaps a few years—before these radio systems would be in use in Britain, and in every police force of any size throughout the world. I felt it my duty to Glasgow to cut out the delay.

I bought one of the radio receivers for fifteen dollars in New York and managed to get some technical details of the transmitting station required to operate it. When I got back to England I sent a letter to each of the foremost radio manufacturers and told them that I was willing to let them have this sample radio to study. They could take it to bits or do whatever they chose to it.

What I wanted was an English-built radio that would do the same job. I said: "It's no use telling me that it cannot be done because here it is for you to see. I know it can be done, for I have seen it work in New York, and I want it in Glasgow."

Soon a radio firm was able to tell me that they could make a satisfactory set and build a radio transmitting station that would send both Morse and speech.

Glasgow's radio-controlled flying squad was the first in Britain to transmit Morse and speech from the same transmitter, and this was a great advance, since transmitters confined to Morse only were never entirely satisfactory.

Another small innovation which was, I think, welcomed, was the fitting of blue-and-white diced bands around the peaked caps of the police officers. Frequently in the past motorists had refused to stop on country roads when they were signalled to do so after dark by an unidentifiable figure in cape and cap—and as a motorist myself I cordially sympathized with them, for there was no way at all of knowing if one was being halted by a *bona fide* policeman or a hold-up man, and one certainly did not wish to risk stopping to find out. White capes seemed impractical, and white caps would not have been sufficiently distinctive. But the "diced band" of the uniform of the Brigade of Guards would be unmistakable and seemed ideal, so I borrowed it for my men and it became known as "Sillitoe's tartan". Since then all the Scottish police forces have adopted the same pattern to distinguish themselves.

Also in the interests of motorists, I attempted to evolve a traffic plan for the city centre. This was certainly necessary, for during rush hours Glasgow's main streets were so blocked by double lines of parked vehicles that they looked like busy garages. But when the Master of Works, Mr. Somers, and I recommended restricted parking there was a storm of protests from the motorists whose welfare we had been so tenderly considering.

I got into trouble also because I insisted that the licensing hours should be observed. I called a meeting of Glasgow publicans and reminded them that the law forbade the selling and consuming of drinks on licensed premises after 10 p.m. It was not by any means the publicans alone who felt that this might, no doubt, be Scottish law, but that it was an intolerable liberty on the part of a Sassenach to enforce it.

Altogether I had been about twelve months in Glasgow before I began to feel that I and my decrees and systems were beginning at last to be accepted with fair tolerance. Gradually references to Sheffield being a "second-rate town" became less frequent; the fact that I had taken a house just outside Glasgow at Kilmacolm instead of in Glasgow itself ceased to be a ground for criticism; and the newspapers reported my doings without adverse comment—indeed, I was occasionally awarded a word or two of praise.

It was some months earlier, however, that the *Glasgow Herald* had championed me most courageously at a time when support for the Chief Constable had not become fashionable. I learned afterwards that for this I was indebted to the editor, Sir Robert Bruce, who remained my friend throughout my stay in the city. A paragraph which appeared in those early days, and which greatly encouraged me, described me as "a man whose high sense of duty has antagonized certain elements in the city . . . He is frequently the butt of music hall comedians and the less scrupulous Press. . . . It is well known that the

Chief Constable's antagonists are on the look-out for the slightest mistake which will help them to further their campaign to undermine Mr. Sillitoe."

The paragraph continued: "Although it is existent to nothing like the extent that it is in America, there is little doubt that a certain amount of 'graft' has poisoned the public life of the city, and Chief Constable Sillitoe has set his face hard against the system, with the result that he has made enemies among those who stood to benefit from a lax administration." This comment was to herald a long and often very discouraging campaign which I had indeed resolved to wage against the most deplorable civic corruption which, I had become aware, was widely prevalent in the city and extended even to certain members of the Corporation.

CHAPTER THIRTEEN

Our campaign against corruption in official quarters – The first successful prosecution – A public inquiry is ordered – The police trap that nearly failed – The final breaking-down of the "graft" system – I receive a knighthood.

GRAFT and dishonesty haunted Glasgow Corporation like a spectre that nobody would swear to having actually seen but everybody felt sure existed. The newspapers conjectured about it, and the ranks of the police were full of rumours. But so far nothing had been done, and nothing could be done about it immediately.

This was certainly by no means because the citizens of Glasgow approved of corruption in the Corporation. But when graft lives in high places, the ordinary, honest man finds his approach blocked from unexpected angles when he tries to tackle it. My own task was not made easier by the fact that I was a stranger to the city.

But I was convinced then, as I am now, that it is one of the worst crimes a man can commit, to use political promises and fine words to work his way into a position of trust and authority, and then abuse it by graft. And one such rotten individual can pollute a hundred otherwise honest men.

It was early in 1933 that we discovered a person prepared to lose a personal advantage so that justice might be done. She was a woman market trader, and she told Detective-Lieutenant Gordon Leith that she had been approached with an offer to move her stall to a much better position in the market. The price of this favour was to be £25, to be shared by two Glasgow bailies (city magistrates). These two men, it seemed, being on the City Markets Committee, could easily use their influence to ensure that a market stallholder should be given unfair preference, and were prepared to do so if they were suitably bribed.

I was so keen to get in my first blow at the corrupt practices of the city that I went personally with Detective-Lieutenant Leith to the bank, and with him arranged for £25 in marked notes to be recorded and handed to us. It was arranged that the woman was to meet the two bailies in a certain café and hand them the money. It was also believed that a third man was involved, who would be present too.

Unfortunately, however, the third man rang up to say that he had been delayed at a meeting in the City Chambers, but was coming right over, and he was warned by the friend who answered the telephone: "Police are here! Trouble!" Whereupon he hung up without more ado—and, I was credibly informed later, staggered white-faced out of the phone box. I fear that meant he never put in an appearance at the rendezvous, and so he managed to avoid arrest.

We were able to secure a conviction against one of the two bailies, a man named James Strain, but the other man was acquitted—there was an element of doubt in the case against him and, as he had been a member of the Corporation for fifteen years and had fought gallantly in the First War, he was allowed the benefit of this doubt.

The result of this case was that the Secretary of State for Scotland, the late Sir Godfrey Collins, ordered a public inquiry into civic graft. But there were too many people concerned in the corruption ring—many of them somewhat reluctantly, I am willing to believe—for our task to be easy, as this meant that there were so many witnesses who dared not speak for fear of incriminating themselves. The inquiry dragged on for several weeks, but eventually fizzled out, with a non-committal and entirely unsatisfactory verdict that there was enough evidence to indicate that corruption probably did exist, but not enough evidence to indicate who was concerned in it, or what might best be done about it.

The police had to wait another eight years before this corruption came near enough to the surface again to be successfully shot at. And this time, the shot set off a chain of surprising explosions.

A minor piece of police routine began the hunt. A police

officer may certainly experience bad luck, but I believe that, if he is doing his job day by day, painstakingly spreading his net, he will also get an occasional lucky break.

Thus it was that after some minor infringement of the licensing laws I had formally to object to a renewal of the liquor licence at the Beresford Hotel, of which Councillor Hugh Fraser was managing director. Mr. Fraser was an honest man. And when his colleague on the Corporation, Bailie Hugh Campbell, approached him with a suggestion that the matter could be squared if the right approaches were made, Mr. Fraser pretended to listen and agree, but as soon as he was able to do so came and told the police about it.

Bailie Hugh Campbell was a member of the Glasgow licensing Bench, and there is no doubt that, with the assistance of similarly corrupt colleagues, he could have contrived that the licence should be renewed, despite any objections the police might raise at the Annual Licensing Court. For this service he asked £120, to be divided between himself and his colleagues.

Two detective officers, Ewing and McIlrick, obtained in marked notes the £120 with which our trap was to be baited, and a listening apparatus was fixed up with a microphone in Mr. Fraser's room wired to the room immediately above. We believed we had done everything most efficiently, but then a conspiracy of misfortunes began to make us look sadly incompetent.

Half an hour before Campbell was due to arrive to collect his graft-money the apparatus was tested again—and it would not work! The receiver had gone dead. Ewing and McIlrick kept cool, and sent a call for police electrical technicians who came round in an Alvis squad car, dismantled everything and hastily reassembled it. The receiver worked no better than before! And by this time there was no more than a few minutes to go before our man arrived.

Well aware that they might never get another chance of catching these grafters, Ewing and McIlrick thought desperately and devised a solution. In Mr. Fraser's office was an inter-com. telephone device. It was quickly tested and found capable of picking up normal conversation within four or five feet. The police electricians rigged this so that it was switched on, even though the keys were apparently turned down—this, in case Campbell might become suspicious if the switch was obviously on to "receive".

In the room upstairs McIlrick sat listening at the telephone extension. The trap was baited and set. Promptly to time Campbell stopped his car outside the Beresford Hotel and came bustling importantly into the vestibule where, of course, nobody knew that police were waiting for him.

"Show me Fraser's room," he said peremptorily to the hall porter. But once again the gods decided to make sport with my unfortunate officers. For the porter, unaccustomed to hearing the managing director spoken of so unceremoniously, misunderstood Campbell, and showed him politely to "The Frazer Room", one of several available for conferences in the hotel. This happened to be the room where McIlrick sat listening to his telephone earpiece, the floor cluttered with bits of microphones, wires, pliers, and all the very obvious apparatus of a listening trap. Apart from that, there were few officers of Glasgow Force with the distinction of looking more like a policeman than McIlrick—who was in any case probably known to Campbell by sight.

Neither Campbell nor McIlrick was in the mood to appreciate this ingenious jest that fate was indulging in at their expense. Campbell fled downstairs and was speeding out of the hotel door when he was stopped by Mr. Fraser who had come to investigate his whereabouts. Campbell gabbled in an undertone about the sight that had greeted him in the Frazer Room. Fraser attempted to reassure him by saying that electricians were testing the house phones, but Campbell's guilty conscience could not be calmed. However, he pulled Fraser outside to his car, and there he took the money, as had been arranged.

At that instant the air-raid siren began to whine. He stuffed the notes into his pocket, and, while Fraser hurried back to the hotel declaring, "He's awa' wi' the money!" he was driving off into the black-out.

The raid was a bad one, but a search warrant was obtained

by first daylight, and Ewing and McIlrick, understandably depressed, arrived at Campbell's house immediately after. Apart from Fraser's word against his own, there was no clue to link him with the corruption accusation except the notes, and the officers were reasonably certain that, after the fright he had received, he would have disposed of them.

However, they knocked at his door. Campbell opened it and let them in. He looked distraught and exhausted, but there were many citizens who looked like that after a heavy air raid. He strongly denied all knowledge of the £120, or the incident of the previous night; he said he had called in at the Beresford Hotel, but on hearing the siren, had left for home almost immediately.

It looked hopeless. But, like the good policemen they were, Ewing and McIlrick did not give up. Scottish tenacity came to their aid, just as it betrayed Campbell. For, in spite of his agitation, he had been determined not to get rid of the incriminating notes, and the officers found them stuffed up a bedroom chimney.

Campbell pleaded guilty to receiving £120 for undertaking to use his influence to procure a renewal of the Beresford Hotel licence, and was sent to prison for six months.

This was a first crack in the edifice of corruption in Glasgow. For when, in Barlinnie Gaol, Campbell was interviewed, he told us enough to enable us to build up a case against three other members of the Glasgow Corporation. One was Thomas Wilson, a round-face, jovial man, retired from successful business, who had entered the Corporation in 1935 and served on the housing, public assistance, gas, and transport committees. He seldom, if ever, raised his voice in debate, but was extremely popular in certain circles, and had been made a magistrate in 1941.

The second member of the graft ring was Joseph Taylor, exactly the opposite of "Old Tom" in style and disposition. Taylor was tall, bespectacled, fiery, and quarrelsome, constantly raising a loud outcry against the "exploitation of the poor". He was the I.L.P. representative of Parkhead Ward, and no sooner had he got his seat in the council chamber than he began to make the sparks fly. He was frequently suspended during council uproars. In 1933 he had defied the Lord Provost after being refused permission to read a certain letter in the council chamber. He had read it at the top of his voice, whilst fending off the attempts of officials to prevent him. In 1937 he had made another memorable scene when he snatched the city's gold mace and stalked out of the council chamber with it, as a gesture against some "exploitation of the working man". In 1938, when he was offered the honour of becoming a city magistrate, he refused haughtily. He was again honoured with the offer in 1940, and this time accepted. If ever there was a champion of justice and valiant defender of the oppressed, you might have thought it was fiery Joe Taylor. It was interesting to note him down in our dossier as No. 2 among the grafters!

The third man on the suspect list was a name already familiar to the police—Bailie Alex Ritchie, who had been found "not guilty" in a case brought against him for corruption in 1933.

Even as we were gathering together the evidence that was to convict these three men, another fissure widened. A Public Baths attendant named George Maguire, having seen what had happened to Campbell, gained courage to come forward and lay an indictment against yet another member of the Corporation.

And this time we knew that we had reached the top. For the man accused by the Baths attendant was no less than Bailie Robert Young Gemmell, convenor of the Police Committee—my Chairman! He also had charge of the Fire Brigade and the City Baths. He and his committee could not, under Scottish police regulations, control promotions in the police force—these were my own responsibility. But they had the unchallenged and final right to authorize promotions in the fire service and among the baths employees.

George Maguire's story was pitiful. When it seemed to him that he was due for promotion he was told by Gemmell, as Superintendent of Ibrox Baths, that promotion, with its increase of pay and status, would cost him £30.

Gemmell was promptly arrested. In his pocket was discovered a slip of paper, showing the names of various persons apparently entitled to receive "cuts" in the promotion graft. In this case, according to the slip of paper, £25 went to Gemmell himself. On 21st August, 1941, he was sentenced to twelve months' imprisonment, and was disqualified for five years from holding any kind of public office.

On 26th September, "Old Tom" Wilson, Joe Taylor, and Alex Ritchie appeared on charges of having solicited and received bribes totalling £225 from the chairman of the Gas Chambers and Coke Ovens Company Limited, Westminster, London, as an inducement or reward for undertaking to use their aid and influence as members of a deputation from the Corporation Committee on Gas Supply, to procure influence for the Company's tender. The money was paid through two Corporation colleagues.

Campbell came from Barlinnie Gaol to give his evidence, and the three wretched men in the dock had an opportunity of realizing what was coming to them. Wilson was sentenced to fifteen months' imprisonment. Ritchie and Taylor got eighteen months each. All were adjudged ineligible for election or appointment to any public office for seven years after their convictions, and were ordered to forfeit their offices as members of the Glasgow Corporation.

Lord Fleming told them: "You have been found guilty of a very grave offence against public morality and good government. Within a period of a few months, this is the third case before this court in which members of the Corporation of Glasgow have been involved."

Almost immediately afterwards, another Glasgow magistrate, Neil Shaw, was sentenced to six months' imprisonment, by Sheriff Kermack at Glasgow Sheriff's Court for receiving £10 for using his influence as a member of the Glasgow Licensing Court. He, too, was barred from public office for seven years.

As a result of these disclosures, Glasgow came perilously near to being disgraced. The Secretary of State for Scotland, the Rt. Hon. Tom Johnston, warned me that if I got any more of that sort of thing and other people were convicted he would have to consider very seriously putting in a Commissioner to act in place of the Corporation.

Fortunately, this drastic and humiliating measure was not necessary. The graft had, it seemed, been broken.

In the following New Year's Honours List I was knighted and the *Glasgow Herald* commented: "Captain Sillitoe's knighthood is a mark of confidence in him by high authorities in Scotland, and their recognition of valuable work of various kinds that he has done, not always in the most encouraging circumstances. The honour is unique in Scotland." My war against graft had been long and had looked hopeless, but at least I had won it in the end and I was very relieved that this was so.

CHAPTER FOURTEEN

The notorious Glasgow gangs – The "Parlour Boys", the "Norman Conks", and the "Billy Boys" – A fight with "Sillitoe's Cossacks" – The valour of Sergeant Morrison – The case of John M'Namee.

NEVER at any time since my departure from Glasgow have I felt that there was any excuse for such men who abused their positions of trust and authority so shamefully. They were not victims of circumstance, and they were driven only by their own unpardonable cupidity to try to extort money for themselves from people in vulnerable positions.

There was not very much excuse for Glasgow's gangsters either, but one should, I think, remember, that while a certain number were violent and unpleasant hooligans, a great many were merely weak-willed, not over-intelligent products of slums and unemployment who drifted into the gangs because their upbringing and poverty and their subsequent enforced idleness had left them bereft of any idea of an alternative means of passing their time and because gang warfare seemed to them to offer a chance to prove to themselves what fine fellows they were.

It is natural for all young people to be ambitious and to feel confident that they are worthy of rising above their fellows. But there are some young men—and young women—who, finding themselves in an apparently inferior position in society, as a result of poverty, lack of opportunity, poor intelligence, or poor appearance (or possibly a combination of all these disadvantages) have not the good sense or strength of character to seek to make something of themselves by constructive effort, but try instead to hoist themselves into the limelight by the flamboyant violence of their wrongdoing. I think that the Glasgow gangs had a great deal in common with the young ruffians who were involved in the Clapham Common stabbing case in 1953 and with the many other present-day hooligans who, without having been involved in murder, are continually perpetrating acts of violence among themselves and against other people. It has been pointed out that a characteristic of many of these present-day young people is their pitiful vanity as displayed in the wearing of weird, ostentatious clothes. This is, of course, a harmless manifestation of the same pathetic exhibitionism that leads them to crime—it is all part of their desire to find a short cut to creating circumstances in which they will be admired and feared by other people.

I do think it is important for those responsible for punishing these young criminals to understand what hopes and fears have led to such apparently incomprehensible and senseless violence. But I also feel most strongly that we should not forget, in our efforts to be fair to the delinquents, that many, many more young people with no greater opportunities in life, manage to-day—as others managed in Glasgow in the 1930's—to live decently and constructively, in many cases making for themselves the opportunities that at first seemed lacking. It is they, far more than the noisy wrong-doers, who deserve sympathy and help, and we should not be so busy cossetting the black sheep that we neglect the white, thereby creating the impression that it is wrong-doing that pays the best dividends.

The Glasgow gangs were born soon after the First World War and it was about 1919 or 1920 that the Redskin and Black Hand gangs became notorious. The childish names are significant, for it was certainly true that the first gang members were not true criminals, but mostly unemployed youths who had lived through the fever of the war without being old enough to take an active part in it. Among them was a sprinkling of older scoundrels who, whether they had done well or badly in the war, were reluctant to settle down to an ordinary way of life that meant finding a job and sticking to it. Most of the gangs simply grew up around their own districts, or just around one particular street corner. When they got up in the mornings the youths had no work to do and nowhere to go except the street corner, where they sat or sprawled on the pavement, gossiped, wrestled, grumbled; and—inevitably —some of them began to scheme up villainies. People who spoke of a group naturally used their meeting place to describe them, and so such names as "the Beehive Corner Boys" afterwards abbreviated to "the Beehive Gang", were coined.

This is roughly how many of the Glasgow gangs began, and how they got their names. They certainly were never, in any sense, organized teams of experienced criminals who grouped themselves round a "master mind".

In 1924 the gangs had become quite well organized, and at this time were undoubtedly ruled by hardened criminals. The more law-abiding or timid members ceased to attend at these significant street corners, the more criminally inclined from other districts were increasingly attracted to them.

The inner circle of the Beehive Gang was composed of housebreakers, and around them moved a much larger group of men who could be called upon to take part in fights, intimidations, and occasionally mob attacks and robberies. The leader of the Beehives was a man named Peter Williamson, powerfully built and in his early twenties. He came from a respectable family, had been well educated according to the standard of the district; and was a highly intelligent and fluent speaker. He could put up a creditable show defending himself in police courts and later in his career was quite frequently given opportunity to do so.

Williamson was the ring-leader responsible for most of the trouble the Beehive Gang got itself into, but he had a quick-witted faculty for spotting the arrival of the police, and by the time the officers of the law had reached the heart of the riot, Peter Williamson was tearfully appealing to the brawling gangs to "behave themselves". This adroit last-minute pose as a peacemaker—usually with the pavement around him littered by the bruised bodies of rival gangsters whom he had coshed— saved Williamson from arrest several times, until he became too well known. He was a dangerous fighter and there were only three other criminals in the Gorbals who were considered capable of holding their own against him.

Williamson's friend and second-in-command was Harry

M'Menemy, who was, however, neither so big nor so shrewd a man as his leader. He was not himself of a calibre to be a gang leader, but he made an ideal lieutenant; he once pleaded guilty to a serious assault that had been committed by Williamson and another gangster named Dan Cronin. M'Menemy was sent to prison on this plea for nine months. Williamson had decided—rightly—that M'Menemy, who had fewer convictions, would probably get off with a much lighter sentence than he himself would have done.

Dan Cronin was not the type to make an efficient gangster. He was a fierce individualist, not answerable to anybody's discipline, and is perhaps better described as a personal friend of Williamson than as a *bona fide* member of the Beehive Gang.

The real brains of the outfit was a man named Howie, who planned and executed numerous clever, ingenious crimes but seldom took part in the unprofitable raids. He was a skilled burglar, and at one time Howie and the "inside circle" of the Beehive Gang teamed up for their robberies with an English safe breaker, who was associated with them for several months.

The fighting qualities of the gang may be assessed from the fact that for a while one of their members—with no great standing among them—was Frank Murphy, who later, as Frank Erne, won the Scottish Welter-weight Boxing Championship and fought Ernie Roderick, to lose a disputed verdict on points. Murphy was quite a decent lad, and did not concern himself with the criminal activities of the gang, but was certainly mixed up in a number of their brawls and battles.

It needed more than fists, however, to become an outstanding fighter among Glasgow "Neds", as the gangsters were known to each other and the police. The favourite weapon in a skirmish was a beer bottle. This had several marked advantages over other weapons. If you carried a gun or knife it was troublesome to be found in possession of it, but a beer bottle could be carried legitimately. It was handy to use as a club, and could be smashed and used devastatingly with its jagged, newly-broken edges, to scalp or disfigure an opponent. In a retreat, or when the enemy fled from close combat, it was an inexpensive missile.

Some of the Glasgow gangsters carried razors, but these weapons were never really popular. It was easier to stun an opponent with a beer bottle, knock him down, and then kick him in the face. When caught at housebreaking, they sometimes assaulted constables with a steel crowbar or "jemmy" that they used for prising open doors and locks.

In 1924 (which was, of course, before I went to Glasgow) there existed a state of open warfare between the "South Side Stickers" and the "San Toy Gang". Besides the two main participants in this "war", there were at least half-a-dozen smaller gangs on each side. One of the most outstanding skirmishes took place when the leader of a small gang, known as "The Parlour Boys", was killed in his headquarters.

The stronghold of the Parlour Boys was the Bedford Parlour Dance Hall in Celtic Street. Their leader was a snub-nosed, sturdy hooligan aged twenty-six, whose name was James Dalziel. Dalziel—or "Razzle-Dazzle" as he was known— scorned so profoundly the delicacies of life that he would dance only with other burly members of his gang, considering it effeminate to dance with girls.

As far as one can reconstruct the scene, the affair began just before midnight on 2nd March, 1924. Rain was deluging down and the dance hall was crowded with the Parlour Boys and their "queens", as the Glasgow gangsters called their "molls" or girl friends. All the gangsters had entered the Bedford Parlour Dance Hall without paying. Their routine was simply to troop through the doorway, wipe their boots, and declare that they "knew the boss". It seemed to be equally important that one should wipe one's boots as that one should "know the boss", and these regulations were to have considerable importance later in the evening.

At about 12.45 the rain was still pouring down outside, when a mob of gangsters belonging to the Bridgegate Boys from Gallowgate, a subsidiary group of the San Toy Gang and a rival faction to the Parlour Boys, came down Celtic Street. It seems probable that they entered the Bedford Dance Hall for no other purpose than to escape from the rain, although they must have been aware that the place was a stronghold of their enemies. They perhaps considered that they might lose face if they passed this chance of shelter merely because it was occupied by their foes.

Whatever their motive, the fact remains that they crowded into the Bedford Dance Hall, delivered the customary formula "we know the boss", and swaggered without further ceremony or payment into the big room where the music was playing.

But Mrs. Stevenson, on duty at the entrance, observed that these newcomers, although similar in appearance and manner to the other gangsters already peaceably on the premises, had omitted one important part of the ritual. They had failed to wipe their boots. She immediately sounded the alarm.

A disgusting and senseless brawl followed, with bottles brandished and knives flashed. Then Razzle staggered towards the door pouring with blood. He had been stabbed in the throat by a gangster named Collins. Various other members of both gangs sustained injuries of various sorts, and a young girl was later taken away on a stretcher. That night the police made several arrests.

To me the most deplorable part of this unsavoury story came later at Glasgow Assizes. A verdict of murder was asked against Collins only, and even this was not upheld by the jury. Collins, who had struck the actual death blow, received no more than twelve months' imprisonment.

The accused men grinned and smirked among themselves, waving from time to time to their friends and admirers who thronged the public galleries. There was no doubt at all that they considered themselves as heroic figures. And they were likely to persist in this delusion as long as they could expect to get only a few months in gaol or a fine (quickly paid on their behalf) for carrying murderous weapons and using them without scruple.

When I arrived in Glasgow, two of the most notorious gangs were the "Norman Conquerors" (known more familiarly as the "Norman Conks"), who came from Norman Street and were Roman Catholics, and the "Billy Boys", who were William of Orange Protestants, taking their name from

Prince William of Orange. These two groups were, of course, bitter enemies.

The leader of the Billy Boys was William Fullerton, who used to work in Gilmour's Club in Olympia Street. Fullerton, I must say, was never a criminal in the accepted sense of the word. He was a fighting man, who undoubtedly derived considerable pleasure and excitement from pitting his gangsters against the Norman Conks, and his generalship was both ingenious and reckless. He left the thieving to others, and his only conviction was for assault. In 1939, incidentally, Fullerton, in common with a number of the other gangsters, joined the Army, and many of them made conscientious and even gallant soldiers. But on my arrival in Glasgow these good records were in the distant future.

The Norman Conks were led by "Bull" Bowman and their favourite weapons were pickshafts, weighing nearly three pounds and measuring forty-two inches in length.

Both gangs used hatchets, swords, and sharpened bicycle chains habitually and these were conveyed to the scenes of their battles by their "queens". This was because they knew that the police dare not interfere with or search a girl, who would at once protest that the officers were improperly assaulting her.

On the night of 19th January 1932, the Communist-inspired group known as the National Unemployed Workers' Movement had organized a parade of Glasgow's unemployed. Bull Bowman, who was just as alert as his arch-enemy in seeking ways of provoking a fight, immediately saw in this demonstration march a wonderful opportunity. He added the strength of his three-hundred-odd gangsters, each equipped with one or two pickshafts. Many also carried beer bottles for fighting at close quarters.

The procession, which was now taken for all practical purposes out of the hands of the Communists and into the direct control of the Norman Conks, turned into Abercrombie Street, which was in the "district" of the Billy Boys.

The police knew about this march as soon as the Billy Boys did, but Fullerton's men lived on the spot and Fullerton managed to get a couple of hundred of them into Abercrombie Street just before the procession arrived. Sgt. Daniel M'Kay and four or five police officers arrived with it.

As the marchers swung into Abercrombie Street, one of the Billy Boys shouted "God Save the King". Immediately eighteen pickshafts were hurled straight at him. Five plate glass windows behind him were smashed. Sgt. Daniel M'Kay, who had been making his way courageously to what he knew would be the storm centre of the battle, was struck full in the face by one of these murderous missiles. Another officer, P.C. William Hughes, had barely time to ward off a pickshaft from his face and several of his finger bones were broken. He had to use his injured hands to protect himself from further blows.

One could feel scant sympathy for the injuries sustained by the members of either of the gangs, for on the whole the provocation was given equally by both. But I deeply resented that my police officers should be constantly involved in these loutish riots in the course of which they were attacked by both sides at once.

There were several arrests and some fines, which were at once paid by levies upon the shopkeepers in that district. The usual technique employed upon shopkeepers who did not choose to contribute was to mix all the shop's goods in a smashed heap on the floor, with the proprietor on top of the pile like a bruised Guy Fawkes. Then as they departed, the gangsters would break his window glass. They could accomplish all this damage in less than ten minutes of entering the shop.

In these circumstances it was scarcely surprising that we went on having riots. The gangsters would assemble around Bridgeton Cross each night, standing in apparently aimless groups, waiting to see what the night would bring. Then after a while they would usually drift off in small parties.

The job of the police at this point was not to interfere with the gangsters as they stood idling, but, when they moved off in one general direction, to telephone Divisional H.Q. with some such message as: "They have gone off towards Carlton"—

which would mean that the night's brawling and destruction was to be carried out in the district of the San Toys.

A regular piece of provocation which we could count on every Sunday was the Billy Boys' church parade. They always marched up Poplar Street and down French Street (on either side of Norman Street and therefore in the heart of their enemies' territory) before turning into the Church of Scotland. This was by no means the most direct route, but they preferred it. Bottles, bricks, and pickshafts would fly like hail from the windows of Norman Street as the "pilgrims" passed on their provocative way. The Billy Boys did not enter the church itself. They felt, apparently, that their job was concluded when they had created the Sunday morning riot. Those ordinary citizens who wished to attend the Church of Scotland in that district faced martyrdom whenever they set out to do so.

Early in 1935, after I had been Chief Constable in Glasgow for four years, Billy Fullerton had another fiendish brainwave. He discovered a most ingenious method of annoying the Norman Conks. He organized a drum and flute band. On all Catholic Saints' and Holy Days he would lead his entire gang, headed by the rowdy band, straight through Norman Street, playing such inflammatory tunes as "The Sash My Father Wore" and "The Battle of the Boyne". Perhaps I exaggerate in saying that he led his band "straight through" Norman Street, for as soon as the distant strains of his offensive music were heard by the Conks, they manned all upper windows, and even the roofs in their street, and when the Billy Boys' band tried to march past, it was met by a downpour of bricks, missiles, buckets of filth, and broken glass. If the Norman Conks could have made boiling lead, I am sure they would not have hesitated to use that, too. It was certainly all that would have been needed to complete the picture of a medieval siege.

The Billy Boys were genuine musicians in a rough way. They played quite recognizable tunes, and before they broke up every night they stood at Bridgeton Cross and solemnly rendered "God Save the King". But in spite of this there came a time when the police felt they would be content to forgo the pleasure of the entertainment they were offered. Chief Inspector James White, in whose district they operated, took the bold step of deciding that the law-abiding citizens of Glasgow had suffered long enough. With my authority, the mounted police were ordered to Celtic Park and two big covered vans were filled with police officers and parked by the roadside. When the Billy Boys' troublesome procession approached, thumping and shrilling on its way to Norman Street, a couple of police officers in uniform attempted to halt it. If the procession had obeyed the officers, the Billy Boys would have met no further trouble but, as we had expected, the police were swept aside. Then the two vans suddenly disgorged their uniformed constables and at the same time the mounted police charged from a side street.

Using their long riot batons, the police scattered the Billy Boys' parade from flute band to tail. The road was littered with casualties and the entire band, together with many of its followers, was arrested and charged with creating a disturbance and assaulting the police. There was, of course, a tremendous outcry against police brutality, and the mounted police were called "Sillitoe's Cossacks", but I was proud to stand by Chief Inspector White in what he did. It was the beginning of the end for the Billy Boys, whose final chapter soon followed this wholesale defeat.

Only one of their men, incidentally, escaped injury. He was Elijah Cooper, the big drum player. When the police charged, Elijah dived into his drum and used it as a shelter until he could surrender peacefully.

As soon as the police of Glasgow realized that they had full support from me in taking the only sort of measures which were likely to be effective in quelling these troublemakers, there was a general toughening in their attitude towards the gangsters.

Police-Sergeant Morrison made an outstanding contribution to the "swan song" of the Billy Boys when he arrested Billy Fullerton in circumstances that I think merit the description "heroic". Morrison was a huge, formidable officer, whose prowess in rough-houses was greatly respected. He was known to the underworld of Glasgow as "Big Tommy from the Toll", his beat being usually around the Toll Gate district in the heart of gangsterland.

On the day that was to prove to be the last of his reign over his rowdies, Billy Fullerton was parading not far from the Toll Gate with thirty or forty of his gang. He was carrying a baby girl of about three years in his arms. Whether or not the child was his own is not clear. It is certain that Billy meant no harm to it, but it was equally certain that Billy was drunk, and since whenever Billy Fullerton walked abroad with his gang there was every likelihood of a violent breach of the peace, with stones and sticks flying, it was clear that the storm centre of the Billy Boys was no safe place for a child to be. The crowd was seen by two young police officers, who attempted to interfere for the child's safety and were roughly handled for their trouble. They were following at a discreet distance behind the gang when they saw Sergeant Morrison. The two officers reported what had happened.

"Let them get round this next corner," said Sergeant Morrison, "and I think from there we shall be able to take care of them." The police station was only about 500 yards straight along from that corner.

As soon as the mob of hilarious, yelling, drink-inflamed Billy Boys rounded the corner, Police-Sergeant Morrison went straight in among them and demanded that Fullerton should put the child down. Fullerton refused. He could not have obeyed without losing prestige before his followers.

"Then I am going to arrest you for being drunk in charge of a child," said Sergeant Morrison, who reached to take the baby from the gang leader. Fullerton hit him, and Sergeant Morrison drew his baton to defend himself. There were, by most conservative estimates, at least ten gangsters to each of the three police officers, who were armed only with their own fists and short regulation-sized batons, whilst the gangsters had an assortment of the hideous and brutal weapons which I have already described.

Hooligan reinforcements poured from nearly every adjacent

house as the battle started, but Police-Sergeant Morrison and his two young officers not only arrested Billy Fullerton on that street corner, but took him 500 yards to the police station through the thick of his own gang. They arrived covered with blood and bruises. Fullerton was charged with assaulting Sergeant Morrison.

It was an amazing sight in court when the gang leader appeared in the dock. All around the court, in the galleries and on the benches, where the witnesses were allowed to sit, there were young men variously disfigured as a result of the previous day's *fracas*.

As each witness of the gang gave his evidence, came the consistently recurring phrase " . . . and then Big Tommy from the Toll hit me, and that is the last I remember". At last the stipendiary magistrate could contain his curiosity no longer. "Who is this Big Tommy from the Toll?" he asked. "If he is in court, will he please stand up."

In complete silence Police-Sergeant Morrison got to his feet, bowed and then sat down again. The stipendiary magistrate looked at the huge officer, nodded and said, "I think I begin to understand. Thank you, Sergeant Morrison."

Billy Fullerton got twelve months' imprisonment, and when he came out he was a broken man. His gang-leading days were definitely ended. Three brave and modest officers, who for four years had watched the well-armed bullies of Bridgeton swaggering and terrorizing, had finally shown what they could do. It was the end of the Billy Boys, and without them the Norman Conks seemed to pine away.

It was, however, the case of John M'Namee which could really be said to have sounded the knell of gangsterdom in Glasgow. His was a most despicable crime, and no one, I think, could hear of it and retain any illusion that these gangsters were romantic dare-devil heroes.

M'Namee and his brother, Andrew, with an accomplice named Kennedy, had threatened a man called M'Allister. John M'Namee and Kennedy each carried knives. Andrew had an iron bar dangling from his wrist and fastened to it by a handkerchief. M'Allister, who was alone against three armed gangsters, said, after they had threatened him, "If that is your way, then we will fight it out man to man, one at a time. There are three of you."

That was a brave challenge, but John M'Namee answered it in one sneering phrase that to my mind sums up the false romance of gangsterdom in Glasgow and anywhere else.

"There are no fair fights here!" said M'Namee. The three ruffians then attacked M'Allister. A passer-by named Angus Doherty ran to help him and was viciously struck down by Andrew M'Namee's iron bludgeon.

At this point the ill-fated Charles Smith, outside whose house the assault was taking place, appeared on the scene. He was coming home from work. He stooped to pick up Doherty who was half-unconscious, and as he did so John M'Namee ran back and plunged his knife into Smith's shoulder blade and through his heart, killing him instantly.

Even after this Doherty would say no more in court to help the police than that he did not know the man who struck him and would not recognize him again.

But, whether or not Doherty was genuinely unable to identify his attacker, there was one witness who could, and did. Fifteen-year-old Mary Smith, standing at the front bedroom window of her home, watching for her father's return, saw him stabbed in the back. She at least was not afraid of gangsters and identified John M'Namee as the man who struck this cowardly blow. She identified him again before Lord Aitcheson in Glasgow High Court on 3rd April 1935, and John M'Namee received gangsterdom's severest sentence for culpable homicide in the city's history up to that date.

As I have already stressed, sentences given in the past had been totally inadequate to act as a deterrent where these crimes of violence were concerned and it was, in fact, as a direct result of the personal appeal that I made to Lord Aitcheson to help us stop such appalling vicious lawlessness, that at last the punishment was brought nearer to fitting the crime. M'Namee managed to escape the death penalty, for his plea of culpable homicide was, fortunately for him, accepted by the Crown.

But he was sent to prison for fifteen years. His brother Andrew got four years and Kennedy three.

After sentencing the three men, Lord Aitcheson said: "I warn you, and those who are minded to follow your example, that the limit of public tolerance has been reached."

This was described in the Glasgow newspapers as "a dramatic challenge to ruffianism in Glasgow". It was a challenge that the gangs of Glasgow did not feel disposed to meet. We had the police well organized and mobile. The public was now whole-heartedly on our side and not afraid to help us. And these heavy sentences were all that we needed. To clean a city of evil, the police must be sure that they have the support of the courts, and that adequate punishment will be inflicted upon guilty men. The criminals and the lawless must know this, too. We knew now in Glasgow, and so did the gangsters, what kind of sentences might be expected in the future.

CHAPTER FIFTEEN

The control of Communist gatherings – Our development of a Fingerprint Department, and the hunt for the "Cinema Bandit" – Police problems in Glasgow – The arrest of I.R.A. conspirators – Gasmask assembly and distribution – Trouble with the L.D.V.

GLASGOW'S mass unemployment made the city a fertile breeding ground for Communist propaganda, and the Communists were never averse to taking advantage of the wretched hopelessness of the unemployed by inflaming their sense of injustice and fanning their distress into active, disorderly rebellion which made conditions harder for everyone and did nobody any good. Mass meetings were held, and every fortnight, when the Corporation met, a procession marched around George Square demanding that deputations be received in the Council Chamber, generally to discuss unemployment relief. At any moment such gatherings were liable to be transformed into alarming riots.

Just after I had taken up my duties in the city, there was a big meeting on Glasgow Green. A man who is to-day a prominent member of the Communist Party was making a highly inflammatory speech against the government. Suddenly, having recognized one or two plain-clothes policemen in the crowd, he shouted: "I see police spies here! You boys know how to handle them!" The officers were attacked by the mob and atrociously injured. One of them was crippled for life. Only the arrival of several uniformed police prevented the crowd from throwing three badly injured and unconscious plainclothes policemen into the Clyde.

I ordered that all future meetings must be conducted in an orderly and law-abiding fashion and I insisted that the processions which marched round and round George Square must be kept under strict police control. I do not feel that this decision of mine was unjustified, for mob-rule had reached a point when it was a most hazardous undertaking for people to attempt to walk across the Square or make their way to Queen Street Station. Anyone rash enough to try to move through the endless procession was practically certain to be manhandled.

The demonstrators carried heavy pickshafts shaped to a bulbous pointed end, and to which was attached a small triangular red flag with the hammer and sickle. When I was taking steps to get the processions under control, I produced one of these lethal weapons to the Parliamentary Under-Secretary of State for Scotland—and I think it did, as I had hoped, convince him that the severe methods I proposed to use were necessary.

I instructed my superintendents in each police division that they would be responsible in future for the proper behaviour of the demonstrators who formed up in their districts. A sufficient number of police officers was told to go with each of the processions as it marched towards the city centre, and to stay with it when it joined the main body in George Square.

Each group of marchers was thus under the control of the police from start to finish, and was kept—so far as we could manage it—in a watertight compartment even at the assembly point. This did result, eventually, in our keeping the mass parades from getting out of hand, for anyone who began to create a disturbance was promptly grabbed and popped into one of the police vans waiting nearby. But, for a long time there were in Glasgow so many thousands of unemployed that the Communists, like the gangs, found it easy to get new recruits.

It was a big and serious problem and before I could solve it I had to have the general public on the side of the police. Fortunately we were getting the police boxes which enabled people to get in touch with us quickly, and a fleet of fast Alvis cars enabled our men to make a swift appearance directly we were aware that a disturbance had started; later we were to have radio to keep the police in touch with each other. And, as I had experienced before, directly ordinary citizens became aware that effective and speedy police action could be relied upon, they were immediately eager to co-operate with us. It was, after all, in their interests, for no law-abiding person would choose to live in daily terror of violent physical attack if he so much as ventured in the streets of his home town. At all events, after a while the startlingly rapid arrival of the police cars—they took no more than five minutes to get to the scene of any disturbance reported in any back street in Glasgow—began to have an effect. Criminals and rowdies both began to feel that the police were everywhere—and, potentially, they were.

I have to admit that on one occasion when demonstrators were marching round and round George Square, I was brought near to ruining my reputation. I had come from the square myself and was waiting in the Council Chamber to hear the Corporation's reply to messages from the leader of the National Unemployed Workers' Movement demanding that a deputation of the unemployed be received there. A prominent member of the I.L.P. began making a violent speech, when suddenly he noticed me in the corner and, pointing angrily, shouted something about "that coward standing there who is responsible for the cowardly, rough treatment of poor, downtrodden people!"

This made me so very angry that for the only time in my entire career as a police officer I came near to losing control of my temper. I went outside into the corridor, determined to wait until the man came out of the Council Chamber and then hit him. I do not suppose he would have objected to settling the matter in such a way, for he was a solidly built man and frequently threatened physical violence to members of the Corporation during debate. But the spectacle of the Chief Constable brawling in the Council Chamber corridor would certainly have been considered a most untoward incident. At the time I was too angry to care.

I waited there, fuming. Then, very fortunately, one of my senior police officers called me downstairs, saying that the mob in the square was becoming dangerously restive. I do not think the officer realized he was protecting me from myself, but in effect he was. Downstairs I had time to cool off, and although I remained angry, I was no longer in danger of committing physical violence to relieve my feelings.

There is a tail-piece to this story, and it has made me feel that if my attempts to prevent the maiming by hooligans of innocent folk, for whose safety I was responsible, were "cowardly, rough treatment of poor, downtrodden people", my actions were at least preferable to those of the fiery I.L.P. member who denounced me. For this man was the Joseph Taylor who, some years later, as I have already related, was one of the eight Glasgow bailies who were found guilty of corrupt practices.

One of my first serious shocks in Glasgow had been the Fingerprint Department. This I found to be the responsibility of an elderly constable who had apparently been chosen for the duty because he was no longer fit for his beat. The department was in a disused police cell. There was a dilapidated camera and some very amateurish developing trays; the rest of the apparatus consisted merely of an inked roller, a pad, and a few dozen forms scattered about. There was no kind of file-index.

I sent the constable to Sheffield to study the Fingerprint System there, which was a highly-efficient reproduction of that at Scotland Yard adapted to the needs of a Borough Force. It became apparent that the officer, who was due to retire shortly, was not likely to be able to undertake efficiently all the work involved, and that was why I asked Sgt. Hammond, my Sheffield fingerprint expert, to come to Glasgow.

By April we had managed to collect about two dozen finger-prints in our files, but nobody else was taking the matter very seriously. Then, on 17th April, Sgt. Hammond (who is now ex-Det.-Supt. Hammond) got his first identification. He had gone, with his usual persistence, to the scene of a house-break-ing and had taken photographs of prints that he found there. He returned to police headquarters, where he had been given an office about the size of a small suburban front parlour, and developed his photographs.

A couple of hours later a surprised and highly indignant thief named Joe Silver found himself arrested for the robbery. He demanded to know what nark had squealed on him, and was horrified to learn that it was his fingerprints that had given him away. Silver had, so far as I can remember, got himself convicted in the previous January, and had only just been released after three months' imprisonment.

We had another identification in May; there were twelve in June; and after that, the Fingerprint Department was well on its way. By the end of its first twelve months Sgt. Hammond and his assistant had secured ninety-six successful identifications.

There was one tantalizing case on Hammond's fingerprint files nearly all that year. It had begun in May of 1932, when the Kingsway Cinema in Glasgow was broken into at 1 a.m. while the watchman was having supper. The safe was robbed of several nights' takings. It was a clever robbery, skilfully carried out. Hammond found a complete set of fingerprints on the safe—this being, of course, in the days before the average burglar had become painfully averse to leaving such mementoes.

Hammond took careful photographs of each of these "dabs", compared them optimistically with the few samples in his record files, and, not surprisingly, failed to find any that matched them. He sent copies of the prints to New Scotland Yard, but they were not known there. Then he put his photographs carefully away, and waited. He had done all that he could for the moment.

Four more cinemas were robbed within a few weeks. At each of them Hammond discovered fragmentary fingerprints that matched tantalizingly with those he had found at the Kingsway Cinema robbery, but he still had no clue as to the identity of the thief who was leaving them.

After this, cinemas were robbed in quick succession at Paisley, Greenock, and Troon. Fingerprints were left each time, but they were as much help to Hammond as blank visiting cards.

Our C.I.D., however, had begun to build up a composite picture of the thief. He was almost certainly a young man, for some of his robberies had involved remarkable athletics in roof climbing. He was able to move from one district to another and stay in each for several weeks. He was probably, therefore, a bachelor—or at least, of no permanent abode.

He had stolen large quantities of cash, and might be expected to be spending it, as criminals do, on gambling, drink, and women; but there were no signs on the race tracks, nor in the kind of public houses customarily frequented by criminals in those districts, and no known orgy of spending after any of these successful robberies.

Then, on 21st January 1933, we got our first constructive lead on the Cinema Bandit. A young man named Gray was staying at the Blythswood Hotel, and had requested to be wakened each morning with a cup of tea. The hotel charge for this service was threepence. On the first day the young fellow drank his tea and left half-a-crown for the waitress who had fetched it. He did this on each successive day, and after almost a week the girl reported it to the manager—who— rightly alarmed by such lavish tipping—told the police.

We investigated this young man speedily and unobtrusively and it became apparent that he did not work, yet he was by no means short of money. He appeared to be a teetotaller and non-gambler.

Sgt. Hammond was very keen to get his fingerprints, but there was no official way in which they could be demanded from the youth. We could not arrest him simply because he tipped half-a-crown a day for his cup of morning tea. I pointed this out to Hammond rather testily.

"Agreed, sir," said Hammond, "but we can 'arrest' the cup of tea, which should have on it all the fingerprints we need!"

Next day a detective waited at the Blythswood Hotel to take the cup and saucer as soon as the waitress bore it gingerly downstairs from the young suspect's bedroom. Sgt. Hammond found a beautiful impression of the left thumb upon the saucer.

It was the Cinema Bandit!

There is a sequel to this story. When he had finished drinking the cup of tea that betrayed him, Gray had left the Blythswood Hotel and bought himself a flashy, powerful new motorbike. This possession could not be confiscated after his arrest, for it was impossible to prove that the money used to buy it had actually been stolen. So, when Gray came out of Barlinnie Gaol, after serving his sentence, he bestrode his motorbike sulkily and rode away in a defiant cloud of dust at an equally defiant and reckless speed. He rode straight into a wall and killed himself.

By 1934 the Fingerprint Department was running so smoothly that when on 16th January of that year, two elderly ladies living in the good-class district of Albert Road discovered burglars escaping through their front door, Det.-Constable James Duncan of the Fingerprint Department was on the scene of the crime almost before their screams had subsided.

On a trinket box he found fingerprints, but the box was patterned with the Royal Stuart tartan, and against this background the fingerprints defied successful photography.

Duncan took the box back to police headquarters, and while Det.-Constable Smith-Liddle, who was in charge of the case, was still typing out his report upon it, Duncan phoned him: "I have been comparing the fingerprints direct from the box," he said, "with the collection here. I think you will find that Mick Ireland is the man you want." (This was not the thief's real name.)

Smith-Liddle went to a tenement in the Gorbals and interviewed Ireland, who was startled at the officer's arrival, but defiant. "He denied it stiff," as the Glasgow crooks say.

Smith-Liddle let his gaze wander with professional alertness around the drab little room and he detected the glint of a ring under the iron bed. He stooped and picked it up. The ring bore the initials of one of the two old ladies who lived in the burgled house. Mick Ireland was so devastated at being arrested within a few minutes of reaching his home that after he had served his eight months' imprisonment he went straight and was never in police hands again.

By the end of 1934 there were 3,935 fingerprints on file in Glasgow; and by 1943 the Main Collection alone held 55,092 prints and showed 5,846 successful identifications during the year.

It was in August of 1934 that I started a Police Gazette in Glasgow as an all-station circular on current crime. This Gazette relieved clerical work and was immediately successful, for in the first twelve months 524 persons were "posted" in it as wanted, and 371 of them were promptly arrested.

In the Police Gazette we did not merely list "wanted persons", but also gave details of registered criminals due for release, and details of their special ways of working. Every crook has his own habitual methods, and will often persistently use the same type of alias. A man who takes a night's lodgings, robs the house, and departs, may change his glib story, and even his appearance, but if it is his *modus operandi* to give himself a high-sounding alias and talk boastingly of his war experiences then you can soon link up a theft carried out by a man calling himself "Major Cholmondeley" with a similar offence by "Colonel Marjoribanks", particularly when both gentlemen are reputed to believe they won the Military Cross at Mons. And if one is described as having a moustache and the other as being clean-shaven, you will, without needing to be unusually imaginative, be able to account for that discrepancy.

The police problems of each new day in Glasgow were a very varied kaleidoscope. There were even glints of humour. I remember the time when a Glasgow citizen came to the police lost property office to report, mumblingly, that he had lost his false teeth. This is surprisingly common in Glasgow, and there was a large and varied stock-in-hand. He was allowed, upon his own request, to try them all to see if any fitted. He spent more than an hour, but was unsuccessful.

Then there was an occasion when two boys, kicking at an old mattress they found in a street, saw something fall from among the mildewed flock. It was a greasy old leather purse, containing £10 in sovereigns. At once we received claims from nearly everybody in the neighbourhood. A bewildered police officer came in, pushing back his helmet to mop his perspiring brow. "I've just been to every household in So-and-so tenement," he said, "and it's a funny thing, Sergeant, but every family has just recently thrown out an old mattress with £10 in it!"

There has been a great deal of talk about Glasgow's methylated spirits drinkers, and we made about ten arrests every week. But I was assured by the Glasgow police surgeons that, for anyone who can stand the taste of it, methylated spirits is probably a healthier drink than whisky. For the record, it consists of pure alcohol, with a dash of boric acid and castor oil, and it is drunk mixed with ginger-ale or cheap red wine.

It was about May 1939 when the Glasgow police began to suspect that their city was being used as supply H.Q. by the I.R.A. The voluble Irish had made the mistake of thinking that any boast or wild word would be safe from consequences if uttered outside the actual boundary of England. It was as a result of taking up the stray end of one such boast that the Glasgow C.I.D. began to keep watch on an assembly hall at No. 132 Trongate. On Sunday morning, 14th May 1939, a number of intent young Irishmen began to gather at this hall, and when it was fairly sure that no more were coming, the C.I.D. raided it. Eight men were arrested, and 540 sticks of gelignite were found stacked in a hiding place under the concert platform of the hall upon which all week an assorted procession of religious speakers, pianists, and politicians had walked, unaware of the sudden death that lay piled within an inch of their heels.

The houses of the arrested men were searched, and 100 more sticks of gelignite were found, as well as 500 detonators, 60 feet of white tape fuse, and a pair of fuse-cutters. These were all identified as having been stolen from an explosives magazine in Garngad Road on 10th May, and from a colliery explosives magazine in Stirlingshire earlier in the year. Four more men were arrested.

It is worth noting that the arrest of the conspirators may well have saved the lives of some of them, for the white fuse they had stolen was "instantaneous fuse", which burnt at the rate of three feet per second. They had mistaken it for the ordinary fuse with a much slower burning rate.

Nine men were freed without trial, but three—Michael James O'Hara, Edward Gill, and John Carson—appeared before Glasgow High Court on 3rd August, charged with offences under the Explosives Act.

O'Hara, it seemed, had made another mistake. He had conveyed a cheap brown suitcase filled with stolen gelignite to the branch headquarters at Liverpool, and had carelessly wrapped some of the explosive in a piece of torn brown paper with part of an address still on it.

The I.R.A. agent in Liverpool, fearing—wrongly, as it happened—that he was being followed by the police, abandoned the suitcase in a back street near Exchange Station. When it was found, Liverpool police read the fragmentary address on the brown paper: "Miss J. Gardner, 37 Duke Street . . ." An officer of Liverpool C.I.D. checked each Duke Street in every city and borough in Britain, and finally decided it was likely to be Duke Street, Glasgow. He was quite correct, for this proved to be the address being used by Michael James O'Hara. The evidence was useful in helping to obtain a conviction, and each of the three men received ten years' penal servitude.

This affair seemed to be interpreted—correctly—by the I.R.A. as a sign that the Scots were not sympathetic to their activities, and had no intention of sheltering them.

A few months before the I.R.A. affair, we had been plunged into the false alarm of the Munich crisis, and air-raid shelters, slit-trenches, and gun emplacements were being hastily dug upon every village green in Scotland.

One afternoon I received a top-priority message instructing me to assemble anti-gas respirators and issue them to the populace. Nobody knew where the respirators were, but we found them, after a search, at Woodside Hall. There were 10,000 of them, to equip all the city's teeming population. But that was all we had. I opened one of the boxes, and found that the respirators were utterly useless as they were. They had been shipped straight from the factory, and needed skilled assembling. We were near to the Maryhill Road, one of Glasgow's toughest districts. I went across to the Seymour Picture House, and persuaded the manager to stop the show. I mounted the platform and, telling them what the job was, I appealed to all girls and women with nimble fingers to leave the show and follow me. More than a hundred of them got up at once. We marched down the Maryhill Road with everybody cheering and singing, and myself at the head of the procession feeling remarkably like a captain of Girl Guides.

They worked with me all afternoon and evening, and before midnight we had completed the assembly of ten thousand respirators, ready for distribution. Those Glasgow lasses worked with a will, and their enthusiasm did not dwindle after that first effort. With the help of more volunteers and of police officers who willingly gave up their leisure hours to assist us, we eventually assembled over 900,000 respirators, and distributed them too, in a matter of weeks.

When war was declared the following year, however, it was over-zealous assistance from the civilian population which caused the greatest headache to the police. Local Defence Volunteers—the predecessors of the Home Guard—saw spies, Fifth Columnists, and invaders in any passing motorist who did not happen to be known to them personally, and they were determined that these scoundrels should not evade capture. Loaded rifles and revolvers were brandished with horrible insouciance at terrified drivers, and gun-muzzles were thrust in at motor-car windows because the L.D.V. imagined dimmed headlamps to be infringing black-out regulations. This was particularly awkward for people driving police and other civil duty cars who were frequently on urgent business. Indeed, one night, after an air-raid warning, I myself was accosted by an L.D.V. who held a loaded rifle fully cocked, pointed at my stomach on Albert Bridge. My identification papers he waved aside, and nothing that either I or Dr. Imrie, the Police Surgeon, who was with me, could say, convinced him that I should be allowed to pass. Police constables in uniform were held up, also, accused of being suspected persons and called upon to produce their identity cards.

In many cases inexperience, panic, and excess zeal were the cause of these antics, but unfortunately a number of quite undesirable characters teamed up with the L.D.V. as well and the situation, apart from being farcical, became quite intolerable. With the agreement of the Lord Provost and the Area Commander I had a police notice published in all the Glasgow newspapers on two consecutive days, giving warning that the police had been instructed to take action when drivers were stopped and threatened for no good reason by irresponsible members of the public, the L.D.V., or A.R.P. Wardens, and I pointed out that, contrary to the apparent belief of the public, masked headlights did not contravene Home Office regulations and could not be seen by enemy aircraft.

My notice greatly annoyed the L.D.V. Area Commander, who demanded its immediate withdrawal. When I had to refuse to withdraw my notice, he wrote very strongly to me, "instructing" me to communicate with Zone I Commander in connection with any cases of incorrect stopping of cars by members of the L.D.V. I replied that as long as Civil Law continued to function within the city of Glasgow I would not accept "instructions" regarding my police duties and responsibilities from any military authority, and any communications I might or might not make were at my discretion. I pointed out that the police had shown great forbearance on many occasions and no proceedings had been taken against any of the people who had been guilty of these foolish and officious acts. I am glad to say that the Area Commander accepted my invitation that he should come and discuss the matter with me and the problem was happily resolved between us. Eventually the trigger-happy L.D.V. became better disciplined and restricted themselves to useful and patriotic duties, and the police could once again patrol without being challenged as enemy agents.

While we were all alarmed and bewildered during those early years of the war, I—in common with most people in Britain—could have no plans for the future. We all lived from day to day, and I thought only of accomplishing to the best of my ability the work which each day presented. At this time I was not dissatisfied with the progress that had been made in Glasgow police conditions since my arrival there in 1931. The radio cars had proved their value over and over again, and not only in attacking crime, but as emergency crowd controllers. They were, for instance, used on the occasion of the launching of the *Queen Mary*. On 1st May 1936 an entirely new police

wireless system was officially opened, covering the area extend-
ing from Fort William in the north to Stranraer and Dumfries
in the south, and from Langholm across to the west coast of
Mull. It served twelve county police forces and ten borough
forces, and was centred on Glasgow headquarters. Then, in
1938, a new police training school was opened in Glasgow,
with accommodation for fifty probationary officers to work,
play, eat and sleep. And, for the first time in all my police
experience, not one complaint was received about food or
accommodation.

As far as my own personal position was concerned, I had
arrived as a stranger and none-too-welcome a stranger at that,
but I felt that in the intervening years I had gained the confidence and goodwill of the public, and also, I believe, the
regard of my colleagues in the police force. If I had needed
proof that the Scots no longer regarded me with suspicion, it
was provided when I received the C.B.E., and later a Knight
Bachelorhood, on the recommendation of the Secretary of
State, Mr. Thomas Johnston, and again, when I was appointed
a Deputy Lieutenant of the City of Glasgow by the Lord
Provost.

In Glasgow, too, we had the joy of seeing our daughter
Audrey married, at St. Mary's Cathedral, in May 1942, to
Surgeon-Commander Robert Spencer Rudland, whom she
had met while she was serving with the W.R.N.S. The cruel-
lest blow that my wife and I ever shared fell on us when
Audrey died with tragic suddenness at the early age of twenty-
nine in June 1950, leaving two lovely little daughters, Susan
and Rosemary.

And yet, though I was now well content with my life in
Glasgow, at the back of my mind there had for some little time
been an unformulated idea that I should be well advised to
think of leaving. As I have observed elsewhere in a somewhat
similar connection, when police work is concerned men must
not stay in jobs until they grow stale. I had done my job in
Glasgow to the best of my ability, but after eleven years there
I felt I had exhausted my ideas. I believed that this great city
and I myself would both benefit from a change.

CHAPTER SIXTEEN

I become Chief Constable of Kent – The amalgamation of ten police forces – "The convoys must go through!" – My plans for a "police village" – The case of the Prime Minister's goldfish and my visit to Chartwell.

B Y the end of 1942, when the losses of Dunkirk had been replaced and Britain was getting ready to strike back, a great invasion army of Allied troops was gathering in Southern England ready to storm the French coast. By virtue of its geographic position, Kent bore much of the burden of this traffic and activity.

The War Cabinet decided that a number of police forces in Southern England should be amalgamated to simplify police administration during the invasion preparations, and I was invited by Mr. Herbert Morrison, then Secretary of State, to become Chief Constable of Kent County Police, and to amalgamate the ten separate police forces in this county.

I was glad to consider this opportunity, for various reasons. First and foremost, I was ripe for a change, and with a total of nearly seventeen years of city life, I was beginning to yearn for the country.

There was no doubt that, war or no war, Kent was still the veritable garden of England. But by this time my wife and I had grown into somewhat seasoned campaigners in the matter of accepting Chief Constableships, so each of us made a mental reservation. My own was that the police headquarters would have to be a building fit to work in, and Dollie's was that the house allotted to the Chief Constable for himself and family must be comfortable and to her liking.

My own memories of Maidstone were not very clearly defined. I had a vague recollection of a market town with narrow streets, and I was sure that there was a county gaol at

Maidstone. I therefore feared that the police offices would either be huddled against the gaol outbuildings, or else that they would be in the cellars of Maidstone's town hall. One or other of these arrangements was regrettably not unusual for provincial police forces.

My wife and I decided to pay an unofficial visit to Maidstone and inspect the premises before we made a formal reply to the invitation. If the house or the police headquarters was a gloomy, cramped, or uninviting place we had decided to turn the offer down, tempting and flattering though it undoubtedly was.

Anyone who knows Maidstone will know how pleasantly surprised we were to be. The police headquarters of Maidstone County Constabulary is one of the handsomest in Britain, and it stood like a modern, airy secondary school, clean and splendid, in twenty-five acres of open, green estate land.

The Chief Constable's house was equally attractive. It had been built less than three years before, and was wonderfully clean and bright. Dollie and I did not need to exchange a word. We knew in that instant what our decision was.

On 1st March 1943, I became Chief Constable of Kent County, with the knowledge that on 1st April the police forces of Canterbury, Rochester, Dover, Folkestone, Gravesend, Maidstone, Margate, Ramsgate, and Tunbridge Wells were to be amalgamated. The Chief Constables of these forces were given the opportunity by the Home Office of continuing to serve, but with subordinate rank, or of retiring on an increased pension. Five of them elected to serve under me, and I had the responsibility of appointing them to their new ranks. I chose four as Assistant Chief Constables, and one as a Divisional Superintendent.

My first big problem was to decide whether this amalgamation should be treated merely as a temporary wartime measure or if it should be based on the belief that it would endure after the war was over. Nobody knew, at this time, what would happen. I conferred with Major Ferguson who—as the new Chief Constable of Sussex—was beginning work upon a similar amalgamation and an identical problem in the neighbouring county.

Major Ferguson's opinion was that it was only a wartime measure, and that we must keep an eye upon the time when we should have to disentangle each of the original small forces from the amalgamated whole and return it to what it had been before. We must, he felt, be careful not to disrupt too much of the original structures of the forces we were absorbing. In other words, he had concluded that the essence of the task was to take the smaller forces in tow, but not take them aboard.

My own decision was exactly opposite. I felt that the amalgamation should be permanent, as Kent obviously lent itself to this new arrangement which would, I was certain, prove to be both more efficient and more economical.

Within a short time I had co-ordinated methods of reporting and administration throughout the county, with the co-ordinating centre at Maidstone; I had approved various promotions and transfers between county and borough forces, and set up a new controlling plan that attempted to incorporate what was the best of each of the old systems. Had I guessed wrongly, it might have been a very difficult task to "unscramble" all this after the end of the war. But it happened that both Ferguson and I were correct in what we decided, for after the war the Sussex force did go back to the pre-war system, and the forces of Kent remained amalgamated.

From the first day I worked with the complete conviction that I was building a permanency. I set up a selection and promotions board to consider the claims and suitability of all officers who—whatever their original parent force—had promotion qualifications. I also took the painful step, which I had taken when I first went to Glasgow, of inviting all senior officers who had reached an age when they could retire upon maximum pension, to do so, and make way in the promotion-list for younger men.

With the kind consent of my successor in Glasgow, I brought Superintendent Deacon (now Chief Superintendent) to organize a Traffic Division, and one of his first moves was to purchase twenty-four vans for £60 each, and put them in thoroughly good order at a cost of less than £40 each. A year later, after we had enjoyed excellent service from every van, he sold them all for £180 each, and used the money to buy another fleet.

Kent was, I considered, too large an area to be successfully patrolled on foot and by bicycle, so we tried out an almost silent motor-bicycle—the Velocette—for patrols, and found it served our purpose wonderfully well.

When I first arrived at Kent County Police Headquarters I found an atmosphere of strange peace. I had immediately nicknamed the place "The Empty Sepulchre" on finding that at 5.30 each Friday evening the entire premises shut down until Monday morning. Soon after my arrival we all seemed to have so much work that our new name for the place was "Banging Doors".

On 17th August we had our part in the first big pre-invasion test—"Exercise Harlequin". I visited every police station in the county and gave them the watchword: "The convoys MUST go through!" I am proud to say that they did. Every road in Kent was surveyed and every bridge measured for height and burden capacity so that as soon as any road became blocked through bombing we had alternative routes immediately available. We changed the security code numbers on our routes daily.

On 13th June 1944 the first flying bomb or "doodle-bug" fell at Greenhithe in Kent. By 1st September the same year, 2,636 doodle-bugs had reached England, and 1,378 of these had fallen in Kent. More than sixty thousand properties were demolished. On 11th September 1944 the V-2 long-range rocket bombs began to arrive and the death-roll mounted rapidly.

Yet the convoys still went through. Many times we had to clear the streets of Ashford while the fuselage of a multi-engined bomber threaded its gigantic, wingless way through the town, almost brushing the house doors.

At Strood, through which the great Stirling bomber wings passed, the streets had to be cleared of all traffic for thirty minutes, whilst at Canterbury it was an unforgettable sight to watch the police officers on traffic duty at Westgate Towers coaxing and shepherding invasion barges through the narrow, tortuous streets, cleared of all other traffic.

To combat doodle-bugs it was eventually decided to put every available anti-aircraft gun in Britain on the Kentish coast. Nearly 400 heavy guns and 600 Bofors guns had to be moved and re-sited. Three thousand miles of telephone cable were laid; 23,000 men and women were moved, and the vehicles of Anti-Aircraft Command travelled $2\frac{3}{4}$ million miles in a week. In four days, despite falling bombs and destroyed roads and bridges, the move to the coast was completed. Soon there were anti-aircraft guns standing wheel to wheel like a steel barricade along all the coast of Kent. They were followed by a similar gigantic procession of barrage balloons.

There was urgent traffic in the other direction too. When the first of the feared Nazi Tiger tanks was captured undestroyed it was brought hastily to England with instructions that it must be rushed through as a Number One military priority, to a certain "boffin" laboratory on the outskirts of London. Every minute was precious. The Tiger tank weighed 115 tons. With its conveying trailer it was 64 feet long, 14 feet 8 inches high, and 11 feet $10\frac{1}{2}$ inches wide. It was routed via Aylesford, and came over the old sixteenth-century stone bridge that the monks of Aylesford had built carefully by hand. It passed, with barely the thickness of a penny to spare on each side. Without fuss and with only the minimum of delay it was hurried through the winding country lanes of Kent, whilst the almost equally urgent unending rush of convoys continued in the opposite direction.

Upon the fields and towns of Kent fell an enormous number of enemy missiles during the war, from booby-trap bombs to V-2 rockets. In their duties, twenty-six police officers were killed and sixty-seven injured. During the evacuation of Dunkirk, I was told, not a single police officer in the county had been to bed for six nights, and during the time I was in Kent there were many other nights when my officers did not sleep. Once I had a phone call from R. C. M. Jenkins, my Assistant Chief Constable and holder of the King's Police Medal. He was in Folkestone. He interrupted himself to mention casually that he could see fourteen flying bombs in the sky at that moment. "But it's all right," he said comfortably, "they all seem to be passing over us—heading for you!"

Folkestone, Dover, and all the coast towns were bombarded by long-range German guns from the French coast. You would see the flash, then there followed a nerve-racking eighty-second wait, while the shell arched its way across the Channel sky, before the explosion.

Under such conditions, my officers carried out their duties. For devotion and gallantry some were decorated. I wish they could all have been, for I know none who did not deserve it. I shall never cease to be proud of having served with the men and women of the Kent Constabulary. And, once again, I would like to make a special mention of the women police, who did invaluable work. When I had arrived, there had been only two, so I obtained authority to recruit a woman inspector, two sergeants, and twenty constables; and to assist me set up this little team the Chief Constable of Leicester very kindly offered to allow Miss Barbara Denis de Vitré, who had worked with me previously in Sheffield, to transfer to Kent. She found that girls from police forces elsewhere who had met with a certain amount of prejudice against women police wished to come to Kent where they would be sure of a welcome. Soon, we had a Women's Auxiliary Police Corps of 179 members, as well as our Regulars, and I certainly never regretted championing them. Barbara de Vitré herself was soon accepted by all the male police; and after her arrival there was little hostility to the idea of women joining the force.

We were surrounded by such beautiful countryside and such excellent grounds at Maidstone, that it seemed only right that we should have a farmyard of our own at police headquarters. Soon I had established pens for ducks, geese, and chickens to help out the rations—if I had had my way we should have had a cow as well, but my colleagues protested that they were none of them adept at milking! An extension of our farmyard, in a sense, was the police canteen. Previously it had served cups of tea only, but, after persuading the Standing Joint Committee to equip us with modern kitchen apparatus, and the services of cooks and waitresses, we soon had an excellent hot meals service available between six in the morning and ten at night.

So pleased was I with our farm and our canteen that I began to think seriously of converting my dream of a "model police village" into a reality. Looking from my office window I could survey fifty-two acres of healthy green fields beyond the actual boundaries of the police grounds and I coveted that land on which to build houses for my married officers. The Police Authority readily agreed to buy the land if it could be obtained for the price fixed by the district valuer. The difficulty was, however, that the owner would not accept this price.

I went to see the landowner, Miss Foster-Clarke, and found her to be a charming and very understanding person. I explained to her what the land was needed for, and she dropped her price at once. So to-day at Maidstone Headquarters there are not only cricket fields, lawn tennis courts, hard courts, football pitches, tree-lined avenues, and flower-gardens for the police and their families, but also the foundations of what is now becoming a spacious and well-designed village of police houses.

I have sometimes been asked how I was always able to get my plans financed with apparently very little trouble. The answer is, no doubt, that I have always been very lucky, and have dealt only with sympathetic and understanding police authorities. But it has also helped when I have been able to show the improvement to be not only necessary but also a long-term economy—as most improvements are. For instance, policemen must have houses, and if houses are not built for them they must be paid lodging allowances, which work out much more expensive over the years. I have, in any case, always insisted that if the authorities want an efficient police force they must expect to have to spend a certain amount of money on it.

Soon after the Prime Minister's return from Yalta, I had the privilege of meeting him—in rather unexpected circumstances. Churchill had been delighted to discover that Roosevelt and he had a hobby in common—that of keeping tropical fish. It seems that Churchill had the better collection and promised

Roosevelt that he would send him several rare breeding specimens as a gift, and instructions were given to Churchill's suppliers to take fish-tanks to Chartwell and select the fish for shipment to Washington.

On their arrival, however, the experts found that Churchill's ponds were all empty. Scores of valuable fish had disappeared.

This news had, of course, to be broken to the great man. I was not there when this was done, naturally, but as a result the Special Branch Officer attached to him had come hot-foot to one of my senior officers and given him to understand that the "Old Man" was, to put it mildly, indignant, to find his fish missing, and that he wanted an explanation.

I decided that it was for me to go and bow my own head to the storm, if such it turned out to be. So I offered to be at the P.M.'s disposal at any time so that we might discuss the case of the missing fish. In due course I was told to report to Chartwell, and got there just as Churchill himself arrived by car from London, dressed in his famous blue siren suit. Very courteously he begged my permission to have a quick meal before he showed me the empty fish ponds. After about fifteen minutes, he was back, smoking one of his cigars. He offered me one—which, incidentally, I took home as a souvenir to present to my two sons, and they each smoked it in turn with great glee.

Churchill treated me with such spontaneous friendliness that I no longer felt any qualms. We made our way to the fish ponds, he assisting me over the muddy patches, since I, unlike him, was not wearing gum-boots and he was most concerned that I should not get my feet wet. When we reached the ponds, he delved in the pocket of his siren suit for a packet of fish-food and threw several handfuls from it to where, had all been well, his fish would have been. But nothing except the spatter of the food disturbed the water. There was obviously nobody at home.

Churchill turned to me, and for a second I expected some acid comment. But he said: "Really, Sillitoe, it is most extraordinarily kind of you, with all your many duties, to find time to come and discuss with me the loss of my fish."

Just as I was replying that it was a great honour to meet him, a grey heron flapped slowly away from a far corner of the ponds. Assuming what I hoped was an expression of great wisdom, I pointed after it. "I think, sir," I said (with some relief), "that we have just seen one of the thieves. You have been robbed by herons."

Churchill drew thoughtfully on his cigar. Then he said: "Yes, I think you are right. And I can quite understand how it happened—after all, there is a war on, and people have much more important things to do than to protect my fish."

The mystery had been solved, even if the explanation did not help matters greatly. We walked back to the house, and he showed me over it, describing and commenting the while in extraordinarily vivid and striking terms. It was an experience I shall never forget. Finally, in his study, he pointed out to me on the wall one of the original Boer War posters advertising his escape as a prisoner of war and offering £25 for his capture.

"That's a very interesting memento, sir," I said. He blinked at the poster. "Twenty-five pounds was damned cheap," he growled, "damned cheap!"

My visit was not, I think, entirely useless, since in the course of my tour of the house I had become very worried about the lack of precautions against burglars, and I warned the P.M. that measures should be taken to improve matters, since Chartwell was an obvious goal for intruders with dubious intentions. He agreed at once, and I am glad to say that there has never been a successful burglary at Chartwell since that time.

CHAPTER SEVENTEEN

I am appointed Director-General of M.I.5 – Some examples of the functions of the Department, and some manifestations of public misconception concerning it.

I HAVE already related the circumstances of my appointment to be Director-General of M.I.5 in 1946. Now I must admit that during my first weeks in the Department I felt myself very much the new boy. It was all very different from being a Chief Constable. Since its earliest beginnings M.I.5 has alternately intrigued and infuriated the public by the aura of "hush-hush" with which it has seemed to be surrounded, and when I joined it I found it so extremely difficult to find out precisely what everyone was doing that I began to feel that its popular reputation was in no way exaggerated.

Some of the blame for my early puzzlement rests, no doubt, with me. I was now among men of a type different from those who had previously worked under me and, instead of a force or team from whom I could expect unquestioning obedience to rules and a scrupulous respect for discipline, I had to attempt to direct a number of highly intelligent, but somewhat introspective individuals, who gave me an initial impression that they were working in a rather withdrawn isolation, each concentrating on his own especial problem. At first I was not very sure how to set about my task. I found myself wondering uneasily what precisely my role was to be. One thing I was certain about—and that was that I had no intention of becoming a mere figurehead. At all events, the first thing was to find out about every aspect of the Department's work.

An important side of this work, for instance, is the maintaining of contact with industrialists—though this may not be realized by many people. A manufacturer might be asked by the Ministry of Supply to make, say, a certain type of

The Duke and Duchess of Kent visit Glasgow, May 1935

Right: At A.R.P. H.Q. with Sir John Anderson, 1940

With my wife, after my investiture, 1942

Discussing the amalgamation of the police forces of Kent County, with three of the police chiefs and Miss de Vitré. Maidstone, 1943

In the photographic laboratory at Maidstone, 1943

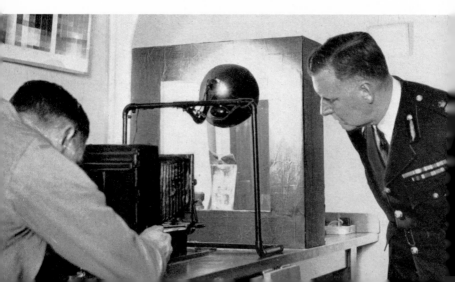

asbestos washer which is to be a component of some secret device. The people working on the manufacture of these washers would have to be prevented from taking them out of the factory—which they might do by accident or acting on some unpredictable impulse, and with no deliberate intention in mind—and from taking snapshots showing their design or the construction of the machinery by which they are made, and so on. And, at the same time, care would have to be taken to avoid arousing in the minds of the workpeople any suspicion that these particular washers had any out-of-the-ordinary interest or value. M.I.5 representatives therefore call on any such manufacturers to advise and warn them, and, generally, to keep a check on any suspicious incidents.

It is, perhaps, worth pointing out that in such circumstances it is sometimes very easy for people to behave in an unexpected way and, while perfectly innocent, to get into a position where it appears that they are acting suspiciously. It is most important, therefore, that suspects should not be arrested without adequate evidence and that the circumstances should be thoroughly and competently investigated by men who are trained not to leap to emotional conclusions based on fragmentary or unreliable evidence.

Since I think that M.I.5 is not usually associated in people's minds with clearing persons wrongfully suspected, I would like to outline a case which was dealt with recently and which was among M.I.5's routine jobs. A Finnish seaman had got drunk in a British coastal district, and had assaulted a woman. When he was arrested he was found not to have his personal papers on him. These were eventually traced to another foreign seaman and it became apparent that some kind of smuggling was being attempted. The second seaman's personal belongings were searched and the police were very disturbed to discover that this man had in his possession photographs which appeared to come from a large industrial organization; they were doubly suspicious because he had from the outset given the impression of being less than ingenuous. So M.I.5 were called in. However, their co-operation quickly established that the seaman, though he might be mixed up in smuggling, was no enemy agent. He had been employed previously doing odd jobs at the dismantling of the British Industries Fair, and it was then that he had made his rather surprising collection of photographs for no more sinister reason than that—in common with many small boys—he liked a mechanical "pin-up".

I find now that my acquaintances cherish a fond belief that it must many times have fallen to my lot to take part in Bulldog Drummond-like adventures in connection with my work in M.I.5. I am sad to disappoint them, though I must confess I have never fancied myself as that type of hero. In fact I had no narrow escapes. Once when I was travelling in the East I found that my briefcase which had been put into bond at Rangoon had been opened by a skeleton key and tampered with before I reclaimed it. But I am not in the habit of travelling around with secret papers in my briefcase, and I fear that whoever had gone to so much trouble to investigate its contents must have been disappointed.

I did, however, suffer a little from not having remained incognito, because wherever I went—and I did travel a great deal during those seven years—I was pounced upon by eager reporters. This I began eventually to dread, for the very simple reason that obviously I could not discuss my business with them and it does become both embarrassing and wearisome to repeat constantly that one is very sorry but one cannot say anything at all—especially when you are well aware that you are disappointing chaps who are only trying to do their own job.

On one occasion when I was returning to this country, I was extremely relieved to find that my exit from the plane at London airport went apparently unnoticed. Reporters were there, but their attention was claimed exclusively by pelicans which had just arrived from Texas. Overjoyed to avoid fruitless questions without any difficulty on this one occasion, I hurried off to my car. But, apparently, I was not to escape so lightly. For a few days later I received a reproachful letter from the Resident Press Committee at the airport denouncing my "cloak and dagger" exits and entrances. I suppose I should have queued up behind the pelicans.

Such routine interrogations by the Press, however, did not really annoy me, but I must confess that when on a holiday in La Baule with my family I found that even in my most trivial leisure pursuits I was still being sleuthed, I did feel a little aggrieved. It so happened that I had gone on holiday just after the disappearance of the diplomats, Burgess and Maclean, and at this time Mrs. Maclean was in the South of France; so it was assumed—most improbably—that I was clumsily disguising my intentions of meeting the lady.

La Baule was full of expectant reporters, staying, unlike myself, in the best hotels. When I and my son were trailed even to a circus—presumably for fear I might come to some understanding with the performing elephant—I felt I could bear my situation no longer and after a few days I cut my holiday short and returned to London.

Incidentally, though I am not at liberty to discuss M.I.5 investigations now any more than I was when I was working in the Department, I feel that it cannot be too strongly stressed that the attitude of certain of the Press towards Mrs. Maclean and towards M.I.5 action in the matter was quite unjustifiable. She had done nothing to warrant her being kept under observation, and no one had any right to prevent her from leaving the country or from going to any place outside it she might choose. And, had she been prevented from so doing, what would have been gained? In so far as the disappearance of the two Foreign Office officials themselves was concerned, I can only emphasize the inescapable truth that no shred of legal evidence has ever been available against either of them which could have served as grounds for the issuing of a warrant for their arrest.

One consequence of any publicity I received at this time was that individual members of the public at least were inspired with confidence in me, though the manifestations of this confidence were not precisely those I should have preferred. I began to receive strange letters—yet in some cases rather touching ones —from bewildered and probably unbalanced people asking me to take charge of their private papers or confiding in me about their personal misfortunes and annoyances, assuring me that they were being shadowed, asking me to meet them under lamp-posts, and so on. An elderly lady sent me her War Savings Certificates and all her private papers, including an acrimonious correspondence she had been exchanging with the Post Office from whose staff she had recently been discharged for reasons of health. "Now that it is in your hands, Sir Percy," she wrote, "I know everything will be all right."

It is not strictly speaking the job of M.I.5 to soothe bewildered old ladies in their private troubles, but we wrote back to her, returning her papers, as kindly as we could, and we arranged that the local welfare and police authorities should keep a friendly eye upon her. For, though one does not wish to encourage such incidents, I have always thought that no government department should treat the public with less courtesy than an individual could be expected to show to another individual.

In other circumstances, however, we always welcomed reports from members of the public who genuinely believed that they had learned of indiscreet leakages of information or of deliberate espionage activities. Often they were mistaken, but frequently we found that someone had indeed been behaving in such a way as to endanger the national safety, though most often it was a result not of deliberate intention but of mental derangement, eccentricity, or mere foolishness. On more than one occasion it was reported to us by a member of the public that he or she had been sitting in a bus or train and had been shocked to observe a fellow passenger reading top secret papers quite openly so that whoever happened to be seated next to him could without effort overlook them. As a result we were able to trace and caution the officials, whether of government department or commercial undertaking, about their indiscretion.

Sometimes exceedingly valuable information is received quite unexpectedly from the public. Some years ago, for example, a man called at Scotland Yard and made a statement in which he alleged that an officer of the Dominions forces on board a ship coming from one of the Commonwealth countries, had, in the course of a flirtation, boasted to his (our informant's) daughter that he had specialized knowledge of a secret military weapon; he had told her that he was on his way to England to take part in the secret testing of it. This report was passed on to M.I.5 and within the next hour the officer had been traced and sent home by the next plane. Nothing was ever heard publicly of this case and the officer was not informed of the reason for his unexpected return to his homeland, but the man who had had the public spirit and the enterprise to make this report, when he could so easily have considered it too much trouble, undoubtedly performed a most useful service to his country.

It is, I think, important for everyone to try and realize that the Department is busy all the time doing such unspectacular defensive work for which, in the nature of things, it cannot hope for credit.

After my first feeling that I was in a job wholly dissimilar from any I had had before, I quite often surprised myself by realizing what comparisons could in fact be made. I was immensely interested to note how science had come to play its part in M.I.5 investigations, just as it had assumed importance in police work. Just one example of this is to be seen in the use and detection of invisible inks.

Oddly enough, it was the conviction of a bookmaker, just after the First World War, which focused British attention on the potentialities of invisible inks. He had thought up quite an ingenious way of tricking his customers: the name of the horse was written in a type of ink which faded rapidly after the betting slip had been handed out, and the name of another horse was written in an invisible ink which became visible when it was exposed to light and air. Thus, the unfortunate punter who backed a horse called, say "In the Pink" would tear up the ticket without looking at it again if that horse did not win. But if "In the Pink" came in first, he would get his slip out and carry it to the bookie—and by the time he arrived to collect his winnings, the name on the slip would no longer be "In the Pink" but—well, probably something like "In the Red"!

Some years before this, however, two German chemists named Dennstedt and Voigtlander had published a survey of secret inks, mentioning, for instance, that messages could be written invisibly in saliva and developed by brushing the paper with a mixture of ink and water. Further progress in the science was marked when messages were written in tannin on brown paper and developed by ironing the brown paper so that the writing appeared in a darker shade of brown. During the 1914–18 war a German agent was captured who had been provided with a collar impregnated with yellow potassium ferrocyanide. He needed only to dip his collar in a glass of water to have a glass of invisible ink, which could be developed into visible blue ink by treatment with a solution of iron salt. Later still it was discovered that writing in quinine could be made to glow visibly when it was put under ultra-violet light.

Here, as in other battles of wits, old methods become useless as they become known to both sides; and new methods are taking their place. M.I.5, like the C.I.D., can never afford to rest on its laurels but must remain always alert to draw at least as much advantage from new scientific developments as do its enemies.

CHAPTER EIGHTEEN

The case of Dr. Klaus Fuchs – The role of M.I.5 in the affair – Its responsibilities and limitations.

ALTHOUGH the bulk of M.I.5 work is accomplished without publicity, the few cases that have been known to the public have revealed at least some of the complexities of present-day espionage. I have explained previously that M.I.5 does not work against any specific foreign power or any group or faction, as such, but is concerned only with taking defensive measures against whomsoever may seek to subvert our institutions or undermine our national security. Inevitably, however, my own experience was concerned mainly with detecting the unprecedentedly elaborate and highly-organized espionage of the Russians and their Communist agents of other nationalities. Among these agents, the most significant from every point of view was undoubtedly Klaus Fuchs. This scientist, who had already started to pass information to the Russians as early as 1942, was finally brought to trial in March 1950. In July 1945, after he had been present at the first explosion of the atomic bomb in the Alamogordo desert, he handed over to another Russian agent in Santa Fé details of the size, contents, and construction of the bomb and of the method of its detonation. All these details he knew, since, as a trusted member of a team of British scientists, he had himself been engaged in work on the atomic bomb as a guest of the United States.

I attended the trial of Klaus Fuchs at the Old Bailey, and, watching that unassuming, unimpressive figure in court, I was shocked and appalled. This single foolish individual had, by a curious trick of fate, found himself in a position to alter the whole balance of world power. With a most presumptuous conviction that his own individual conscience could guide him more wisely than the precepts of laws which govern the whole

British people, and indeed all human conduct, he had taken upon himself to betray the faith and loyalty not only of his personal friends but also of the country which had befriended him and shown him hospitality when he was in need of it.

The charge against him was not high treason, for this can be made only against a man who betrays his country to another with which it is at war. Since we were not at war with Russia, Fuchs escaped the death penalty, but he was sentenced by the Lord Chief Justice to the maximum punishment for passing secret information to a foreign power—fourteen years' imprisonment.

Fuchs was responsible for espionage, the results of which were most momentous. But, as he himself explained, it was as if he had described a motor-car, yet not given details of the carburettor or electrical system; for such was the secrecy surrounding the construction of the bomb that it was as if a motor-car was being invented by groups of men working separately and in isolation on its various parts, none of them being entirely certain of the secrets of the others.

This does not alter the fact that the treacheries of A-bomb scientists cost the democracies a great deal. It may even be—I do not know—that had it not been for the several traitors who betrayed British and American secrets, Russia might not even yet have succeeded in developing the atom bomb to a point even approaching potential use.

In the case of Fuchs, the circumstances were unusual. He was born in Germany and his youth was spent in the troubled postwar period of upheaval. His father was a Lutheran clergyman who became a Quaker and taught his two sons and two daughters firmly that it was not enough to know what was right, but that one must always act according to one's conscience, no matter what the cost.

The result of this teaching, when it coincided with the Nazi régime, was that one daughter committed suicide after Nazi persecution, another daughter and the elder son were driven into exile, and the younger son—Klaus—had to go underground to hide from the Brownshirts among the Communists. The good clergyman's wife committed suicide and the pastor himself was thrown into prison. Those were unhealthy days, in Germany, for men, women, and children who possessed independent consciences.

Klaus Fuchs had, whilst a student at Kiel University, crossed swords with the Nazi Party and had published a pamphlet when he was twenty years old, condemning it. The next year Hitler became Chancellor, and the Nazi students in Kiel joined up with the Brownshirts in a victory parade before the classrooms. Klaus Fuchs chose that moment to walk out amongst them and damn them to their faces. He was lucky not to be killed, but he was savagely beaten and flung into the river.

At that time the only party in Germany that did anything at all to oppose the Nazis was the Communist Party. Klaus Fuchs joined it, and wore the hammer-and-sickle badge boldly in his lapel until he knew the Gestapo were after him; then he pinned it inside his jacket and became a member of the anti-Nazi resistance group.

Fuchs was exceptional in the extent of the damage he did, but he was not alone in the dilemma which resulted in his treachery. When he betrayed the atomic secrets to Russia, he did so because he believed sincerely that the Communist way of life was more admirable than our own. It was at first as a matter of simple conviction that he decided to place his own scientific findings at the disposal of the Russians, thinking them worthy recipients of his knowledge. His position became more and more complicated as the information at his disposal grew increasingly important and he realized that his giving or withholding of it might substantially alter the fate of all the peoples of the world. He was exceptional in having such information to dispose of, yet one must recognize that in the workings of his mind which persuaded him that he was justified in disposing of it against the interests of his adopted country, he was not alone. Since the end of the last war M.I.5 has been constantly aware that in this country it is by no means impossible for men in positions of trust and authority to become enamoured of Communist doctrine to the point where they will spy on behalf of the Russians and feel no shame in doing so.

These men who betrayed us were unlike any earlier spies or traitors in history. They did not want money, nor personal glory, nor were they lured into espionage for any reasons of adventure, so far as one can see. They were men who had come via the quiet and unpurposeful ways of scholarship into sudden possession of powerful, terrible knowledge. By their very remoteness from the ordinary human ways of life and the struggles and bewilderments of their neighbours, these men were lured to make the mistake of thinking that they and their private decisions were beyond our ordinary law. It was the same with Fuchs as with Dr. Nunn May; although these two men were markedly different in personality, each felt that he was not to be bound by any declarations made under the Official Secrets Act, nor to be swayed by any emotions such as normal loves and loyalties.

The Fuchs family was not Jewish. But Pastor Fuchs, his elder son and two daughters organized escapes for Jewish refugees from Nazi terrorism. Eventually, they had to scatter and flee. In Berlin, Klaus Fuchs, the younger son, was advised by the anti-Nazis to escape from Germany and continue his studies abroad, so that he could return one day to help rebuild his country when Hitler had fallen from power.

Fuchs, aged twenty-one, arrived in England, ragged, pale, and hungry, with all his property in a small canvas bag, on 24th September 1933, and was registered as an alien—one of hundreds who were arriving daily. Fourteen months later the German consulate at Bristol reported unofficially to the Bristol police that Fuchs was a Communist, wanted by the Gestapo.

This information was correctly passed by the Bristol police to London, with the comment of the Chief Constable that Fuchs, as an alien, had been checked three times at intervals, was behaving himself, and was not taking any part in Communist activities in Bristol.

The British security authorities were at this time taking a somewhat cynical view of such Gestapo denunciations, for it was Nazi practice to declare almost every refugee a Communist, and to agitate for him to be sent back to Germany if the man were at all important. The only variation was for them to accuse a refugee of being a wanted criminal. In the case of Fuchs, they did not demand his return nor brand him a criminal. By comparison with many other Gestapo incriminations, young Fuchs's denunciation was very mild.

For the next six years Fuchs lived a withdrawn, studious life with Quaker families in England, and was assisted by the Society for the Protection of Science and Learning to complete the studies that had been so violently interrupted at Kiel. He went first to Bristol University upon a scholarship grant, and afterwards to Edinburgh, where he won the Carnegie Research Scholarship. All this time—and up to 1939—there was an unrestricted and eager interchange of reports between the scientists of every nation of the world, upon progress in nuclear physics.

In July 1939 Fuchs applied for British naturalization, probably not so much because of any overwhelming loyalty at this time to us, but because life as an alien held certain disadvantages. Before naturalization could be granted, however, war was declared and after two months he was brought before the Aliens' Tribunal at Edinburgh for investigation. Contrary to suggestions that have since been made, he did not declare any Communist sympathies before this Tribunal, nor did he say that he had at any time been a member of the Party. His excellent record whilst in Britain ensured that he was permitted to return to his work at the university.

But at the Dunkirk crisis Fuchs was scooped into internment with thousands of other refugees from Nazidom. He was sent first to the Isle of Man, and thence to Canada, under what were, beyond denial, conditions of extreme haste and discomfort. Unfortunately the Canadians were ill-informed as to the precise status of these internees, and subjected them to somewhat contemptuous treatment, believing them to be Nazi spies. Fuchs, wearing the uniform of a prisoner of war with a big coloured patch on the back, was by further mischance sent to a camp for particularly belligerent Nazis. It was January 1941 before his scientist and university friends obtained his release and he was able to return to England, where he joined Professor Peierls at Birmingham in the first wartime research upon the atomic bomb.

The salary was £275 a year, and Fuchs was not told more about the job than that it was urgent, secret, and had to do with the war effort. He accepted the post, and Professor Peierls applied to the department concerned—the Ministry of Aircraft Production—for authority to employ him. The report of M.I.5 was required, but all the Department knew that might be significant was that the Gestapo had said several years before that he was wanted as a Communist. He had been seven years in England without flaw in his behaviour, and had applied for naturalization. He was a proven enemy of the Nazis, and the war we were fighting at that time was against nobody but the Nazis and their friends. The security advice given on Fuchs was that he was an acceptable risk on a low security rating, to have restricted access to confidential information.

It is not the job of M.I.5 to dictate whether or not a man or woman shall be given a particular job. M.I.5 merely advises the government department concerned, and requires to have a final say in such decisions only when candidates for M.I.5 itself are being considered.

At this time Mr. Churchill and his Cabinet had stated most emphatically that anybody who could help us win the war should be employed. So Fuchs was employed.

He signed the declaration required by the Official Secrets Act and at this point loses all logical claim to sympathy for what he afterwards did. For the present, however, he worked under Professor Peierls, living in his household; and he continued to do so without incident or any suspicious action, for the next two years. The Peierls sewed on his buttons and helped him buy his Christmas gifts, and sent his shoes for repair; occasionally they took him to the cinema, but usually he came straight from the laboratory to his bedroom where he continued to work until midnight.

After six months, another great wartime secret came into being. It was the "firm" registered as Tube Alloys, and in reality it was the clearing house for atomic bomb research. The head of staff was Sir Wallace Akers of Imperial Chemical

Industries, who was directly answerable to Sir John Anderson and the Prime Minister, and whose job it was to co-ordinate work on the atom bomb at the various laboratories and secret research plants. All the scientists at Oxford, Cambridge, Birmingham, Edinburgh, and elsewhere, were to send in monthly reports so that the main effort could be clarified and no work wasted or duplicated.

One man became outstanding. One man sent in reports punctually, never pleading petulantly that he was too busy. Always his reports were models of clear thinking, accuracy, and simplicity, despite the deep and abstruse subjects he was exploring. And whenever called upon to explain his reports to scientists and others engaged in different lines of work, he showed a remarkable flair for reducing them to simple, easily understandable language. This man was Dr. Klaus Fuchs, among the youngest of the scientists who had now come to the forefront in the vital work of separating uranium isotopes, and by 1942 he had become recognized throughout Britain and America as a scientist who excelled at solving intricate problems, and whose results could be utterly depended upon.

It became essential to introduce Fuchs to most secret matters, so that his work would not be wasted. No alien could be permitted to see the relevant papers, so it would be necessary for him to be naturalized. The Tube Alloys directorate, answerable, as it was, directly to the Lord President of the Council and the Prime Minister, pressed strongly for this naturalization to be granted without delay.

On 7th August 1942 Fuchs took the oath of allegiance to the Crown, and became British by naturalization. At this time he was already passing information to the Russians, in the belief that they, being enemies of his bitter foes the Nazis, were also entitled to such information. He had made contact with Simon Kremer, who was secretary to the Soviet Military Attaché in London—although Fuchs knew only his code name, "Alexander", and that he belonged to the Russian Intelligence Service. By this time Hitler had turned his armies to attack Russia, and Fuchs began to give the Russians carbon copies of reports which he had typed, or the original pencil manuscripts from which the typescripts were made. At first, he gave them only the results of his own brainwork, for in this way his conscience was clear. But this mental reservation did not last very long, and he was soon giving them all the information he could get, which was considerable.

He used to meet a woman agent of the Russian Intelligence Service in Banbury, and continued to do so until he went to the United States for the final, fateful chapter of the work upon the atom bomb.

The strange thing is that although Fuchs was giving information to a foreign power, he was also doing original work for us that was of immense value. His thesis upon the control of a diffusion cascade is accepted by many scientists as having been one of the crucial keys to the solution by British and American scientists of the main constructional problem of the bomb.

I think it only fair to the security services of the United States to make it absolutely clear that when Fuchs landed in New York and went immediately to Washington with the other members of the British mission, he was not subjected to any further investigation by the Americans, but was accepted as a fully accredited and trustworthy person. He was required only to sign the formal security undertaking with the United States Government.

We were well aware in 1949 that there was a traitor in our citadel of atomic research. From the inquiries we made it was soon established that the traitor must be the man who was then head of the Theoretical Physics Division at Harwell Research Station—Dr. Klaus Fuchs.

Now, as so often happens in counter-espionage, we had identified our man but were not able to prove anything against him. Intelligence information is one thing; legal evidence sufficient to justify prosecution is another.

The only procedure in such cases is to acquire knowledge about the man himself, for if we know his motives and his state of mind we may then be able to extract from him by skilled interrogation the evidence we need.

Fuchs was not a spy of the story-book variety, any more than Nunn May had been. They were both ideological traitors who commanded, through their own knowledge, power vastly disproportionate to their positions in the world. They are psychological and political phenomena of the twentieth century. The existence of such persons greatly eases the task of the Russian Intelligence Services in making high-grade contacts to probe into our most secret sources of information on defence.

You can send a man into an enemy country easily enough. But he will not be much good to you until he has contacted people who will give him the information he seeks. There have been very few countries who enjoyed such good fortune as do the Russians in their espionage, for such men as Fuchs and Nunn May who already had their contacts were apparently prepared to come forward and seek out the Russians to give information to them.

Such a man as Fuchs was a product of the chaotic political conditions of the age. His first foe had been Nazism, and in those days the Russians were the opponents of Nazism, though they found it easy enough to switch over with Oriental blandness and embrace the friendship of Hitler when it suited them; but such men as Fuchs could not make such chameleon-like changes.

However, whilst he was acting as a willing and eager spy for Russia and facing considerable danger on their behalf, he was becoming increasingly aware of the democratic way of life. He made friends in England and began to acquire loyalties to them, and through them he developed a loyalty to Britain.

After the first atomic bomb explosion, there was nothing to stop Fuchs from escaping to Russia—except his own decision to stay with us, the people of his adoption, because he preferred to do so even though he risked exposure as a spy and the resultant inevitable punishment.

Living amongst us did for Fuchs what life in Canada did for Gouzenko. From having been morose, introspective, and fanatical, Dr. Fuchs at Harwell was well upon the road to becoming warm, friendly, and generous. The Communists had taken from him all that he could give, but they had given him nothing in return except £100 that he did not want. They gave him neither friendship, affection, nor hope for the future, but in England he found all these things, and in America, too, he found them. Fuchs, when he lived amongst the men and women of the democratic world, was completely won over by them. It was too late to save the secret of the atom bomb. But, because he was already in so deeply with the enemy, I think we can claim that the ultimate victory was for this reason all the more important and significant.

When we began to study Fuchs's personality in 1949 it became apparent that he was undergoing a deep crisis of conscience and that if he were approached with an appeal to that conscience there was some hope of being able to complete this process of conversion.

It was with this hope in mind that William Skardon carried out his interrogation on behalf of M.I.5; it was carried out patiently and with considerable understanding of Fuchs's state of mind.

I think that the facts, firstly, that this method was ultimately successful, and, secondly, that at no time was any resort made to the methods of interrogation that are notoriously used behind the Iron Curtain, provided the most interesting and hopeful aspect of the Fuchs case.

It proved that the weapons of the free world—the weapons of freedom and truth—are effective ones in the problems of to-day. Simply by living amongst us and observing our way of life and assessing our democratic values Fuchs became converted and willingly and deliberately stepped down from his pedestal as the man who held the key to world power. He exchanged this position for that of a prisoner in a British prison, because his conscience told him that this grim course was the better and the nobler one to take.

One result of the eventual arrest of Fuchs was that, not unnaturally, the American Federal Bureau of Investigation was anxious to obtain from him any information which might be of assistance to them. Mr. J. Edgar Hoover therefore sent over to this country two of his senior agents who arrived with the request that they should interview Fuchs. Now it is, of course, the law in this country that no British subject can be interrogated before his trial, and I had to explain this. The interview

Klaus Fuchs

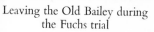
Leaving the Old Bailey during
the Fuchs trial

William Skardon and Wing-Cmdr. Henry Arnold

Professor Enrico Fermi with Bruno Pontecorvo in Italy in 1950

At a Press Conference in America, 1951

My farewell visit to
No. 10 Downing Street, 1953

could, nevertheless, be permitted after the trial, subject to Fuchs's acquiescence. It so happened that he was then entirely co-operative in giving the F.B.I. information and this led eventually to the arrest of American citizens also engaged in espionage.

I myself visited Hoover in this connection and was always most cordially welcomed. I have a most sincere admiration for the extraordinarily efficient organization he has built up—an organization which is characterized by his own personal qualities of uncompromising honesty and upright incorruptibility both in great and small matters. It was with very great pleasure that I was privileged to be present at the occasion in Washington when, in recognition of the great services of the F.B.I. in the common cause of Great Britain and the United States, its chief was created a K.B.E.

CHAPTER NINETEEN

Mr. Attlee's statement to the House concerning Fuchs and the
security services – The disappearance of Bruno Pontecorvo – The
impossibility of taking action without evidence.

I CONSIDER that I was most fortunate in having the privilege
of working under Mr. Attlee, a man whose unfailing kindness and consideration I could always rely upon. M.I.5 came
in for a certain amount of criticism from the public and the
Press during my term of office. The greatest outcry was probably in connection with the Fuchs case, and I should like to
quote a statement made by Mr. Attlee in the House of Com-
mons on 6th March 1950:

". . . I want to say one word about a matter which has
caused a good deal of writing in the Press, and that is the
Fuchs case. It is a most deplorable and unfortunate incident.
Here we had a refugee from Nazi tyranny, hospitably enter-
tained, who was secretly working against the safety of this
country. I say 'secretly' because there is a great deal of loose
talk in the Press suggesting inefficiency on the part of the
Security Services. I entirely deny that. Not long after this
man came into this country—that was in 1933—it was said
that he was a Communist. The source of that information
was the Gestapo. At that time, the Gestapo accused everybody of being a Communist. When the matter was looked
into there was no support for it whatever. And from that
time onwards there was no support. A proper watch was
kept at intervals. He was a brilliant scientist. He was taken
on in 1941 for special work by the Ministry of Aircraft
Production. He was transferred to the Department of
Scientific and Industrial Research. He went to America.
He came back to Harwell. On all those occasions all the

proper inquiries were made and there was nothing to be brought against him. His intimate friends never had any suspicion. The universities for which he worked had the highest opinion of his work and of his character. In the autumn of last year information came from the United States suggesting there had been some leakage while the British Mission, of which Fuchs was a member, was in the United States. This information did not point to any individual. The Security Services got to work with great energy and were, as the House knows, successful. I take full responsibility for the efficiency of the Security Services and I am satisfied that, unless we had here the kind of secret police they have in totalitarian countries, and employed their methods, which are reprobated rightly by everyone in this country, there was no means by which we could have found out about this man.

I do not think there is anything that can cast the slightest slur on the Security Services. Indeed, I think they acted promptly and effectively as soon as there was any line which they could follow. I say that because it is very easy when a thing like this occurs—it was an appalling thing to have happened—to make assertions. I do not think that any blame for what occurred attaches either to the Government or to any of the officials. I think we had here quite an extraordinary and exceptional case. I mention that because of the attacks that have been made. . . ."

There are, I would say, two classes of criticism that have been directed at the Department. Firstly, alleging that we have not done our duty well enough—as in the Fuchs case—and, secondly, objecting that we have not done at all certain things which the public in moments of emotion conceive should have been our duty. In so far as the first criticism is concerned, I would not dream of denying that M.I.5 was mistaken about Fuchs, and that it would have been much more laudable had the Department been able to establish—or even merely to suspect—in 1942 instead of in 1949 that Fuchs was passing information to the Russians.

But, having said that, I would like to point out that M.I.5 is not a supernatural organization. I have sometimes felt that many people, not knowing accurately what its methods are, have come to expect that its representatives must all be endowed with a sixth sense. The fact is that there was absolutely no valid reason why anyone's suspicions should reasonably have been aroused about Fuchs. I have stated the position concerning him: he had been a Communist many years before in Germany, where being a Communist was almost the only alternative for a politically conscious, but immature, young man opposed to Hitler's régime. At that time, it was his opposition to Nazism that seemed significant to us; and it was still significant when he was given his job in the Ministry of Aircraft Production in 1941. He had done absolutely nothing then to suggest that he was still a Communist sympathizer; and, in any case, Russia was our ally in the war against Germany. If, now, a man is known to be an ardent Francophile or to have unusually friendly relations with American citizens, we should hardly be inclined to consider that a reason for regarding him with suspicion.

Given, then, that we had never had any grounds for suspecting Fuchs, what should we have done? Should we have, all the same, arranged for him to be shadowed night and day? In that case we should have had logically to follow the same procedure in the case of all the other apparently quite innocent men who were engaged on secret work—and their number was fairly large. One must consider what, if we had done that, such shadowing would have entailed. It is not just a simple matter of detailing one man to follow another. Just imagine the movements of an ordinary individual—he jumps on buses, visits friends, travels in tube trains, mingles with crowds, changes his mind about which way he is going, speaks to hundreds of people, receives guests, goes on holiday—and all the time you are expecting your sleuth to keep sight of him. He has no way of knowing if any slight action or gesture on the part of his quarry has any particular significance. Besides that, a man who notices another man two or three times standing near him—perhaps on a deserted railway platform or in other conspicuous circumstances—soon begins to ponder on the coincidence. The shadower would therefore have constantly to be replaced by another man, if suspicion were not to be aroused. It would be necessary to employ whole battalions of men to keep a foolproof track of just one solitary scientist.

Apart from the obvious practical impossibility of employing such tactics, inevitably some of the scientists would come to sense or somehow suspect that they were being watched. And then you would have a violent outcry, for these men, ninety-nine per cent at least of whom would be entirely blameless, would, very reasonably, protest most strongly. Their lives would have become a nightmare once they realized that their every action was being spied upon, and pretty soon they would probably be wondering whether it would not be preferable to risk the remote possibility of being killed in a future war because of a leakage of information rather than live under such unspeakable conditions.

Moreover, if the police were constantly making arrests because, in the general atmosphere of suspicion, they became convinced that a scientist handing over, say, a parcel of laundry was probably communicating with a foreign power, wrongful and probably outrageously unwarranted arrests would become notorious. I think that anyone who seriously considers what he is really advocating when he criticizes M.I.5 "inefficiency" in such respects will see that he is advocating more than he in fact intended.

With regard to the second type of criticism, I have already referred to public concern about the disappearance of the Foreign Office officials, Burgess and Maclean. There was also manifest great dissatisfaction among the public when Bruno Pontecorvo, another scientist who had previously been working at Harwell, failed to return to this country after a holiday in Italy. He was known to have taken a plane to Helsinki, and from that point no more has been seen of him in the Western world.

The public concluded that he had gone to Russia. Assuming that this be so, what could M.I.5 have done in the matter? "He should have been stopped from going to Russia," was the cry. But in this country a man cannot be arrested unless there is legal evidence to warrant it. Even if he *were* arrested on the grounds of reasonable suspicions, he would have to be brought for trial, and such evidence would have to be produced then, or he would be set free again immediately. He would thus become just as much at liberty as he had been before to leave the country. The only difference would be that, given that he were in fact an espionage agent, he would thenceforward be more than ever on his guard against giving anything away to the authorities—or else he would be more than ever anxious to escape to Russia while the going was still good!

As I have tried to explain, it is quite possible for the Department to have intelligence information which makes it reasonably sure that a man is an espionage agent without being able to produce legal evidence against him. An easily understandable parallel would be if someone told the police that he had overheard a man whom he knew mentioning to a friend that he had committed a robbery. It might well be true that the man had committed the robbery, but unless the police could get more evidence of it than the unsubstantiated word of one man claiming to have overheard a conversation, they would look extremely silly in court if they charged him with the crime. No jury would convict on such slight grounds, and the man, who would, presumably, deny the charge fiercely, would be very likely to have proceedings taken against the police for wrongful arrest.

M.I.5 has, I repeat, no executive powers of its own. And the head of the Security Service is—fortunately—not empowered to take the law into his own hands and put people under arrest because he suspects them of being spies, or for any other reason. If he were so empowered, what a terrifying prospect that would be! It would mean that if it happened that the head of the Security Service were dishonourable enough to use his position for his own purposes—to dispose of his enemies, for instance—he could, on any trumped-up charges of suspicious behaviour, keep whomsoever he pleased under lock and key indefinitely at his own pleasure. He is responsible to no one but a Minister, and it is not inconceivable that the Minister might be easily convinced that he was acting in the interests of the State. Without our hypothetical head of the Security Service being a real rogue, moreover, he might be swayed by all sorts of personal prejudices, and if he were able to follow no law but his own personal conscience and judgment, that might work out very unpleasantly for innocent people who were unfortunate enough to have displeased him in some way by their beliefs, their habits—or merely by their personal characters.

Incidentally, I should like to dwell for a moment on this matter of acting according to one's own conscience. It is a complex problem. As the Fuchs case demonstrated most poignantly, a man may be very sincere according to his own lights—but those lights may be dim, or they may shine in one direction only. I do not think that a man who is in any way responsible for the administration of the law is entitled to be guided by his own fallible conscience alone; in my opinion, he should defer in all things to the law as it has been formulated by the collective wisdom of the community.

It is, I think, most vitally important that we should all bear in mind that if we cry out against the people who have abused their liberty in this country, we must remember that had we deprived them of that liberty without legal evidence against them we should have been taking steps which would, inevitably, have threatened the liberty of every one of us in Britain. We should, in fact, have been standing at the top of the slippery slope which leads to the setting up of a "Police State"—in which the ordinary citizen goes in constant, helpless fear of a Secret Police against whose decrees he has no redress. Surely, we none of us want that? I, myself, at any rate, would rather see two or three traitors slip through the net of the Security Service than be a party to the taking of measures which would be calculated to result in such a régime.

CHAPTER TWENTY

An account of two "minor" spies – William Marshall and Tony Dewick.

IT might appear that when men of the calibre of Klaus Fuchs are found to act as Communist spies, the Russians might scorn very small fry. I should like, therefore, to relate the story of a rather pitiable young man who, though he was not in a position seriously to harm his country by his treachery, was seduced by Russian blandishments until he was perfectly prepared to do his best to advance the Russian cause to the detriment of Britain. I find the case of interest for it demonstrates that individual self-interest and quirks of character can lead very ordinary people into the most unpredictable situations.

The case of William Martin Marshall was tried at the Old Bailey on 10th July 1952, and this young man, the son of a London bus driver, was sentenced to five years' imprisonment for offences under the Official Secrets Act. He had been arrested in King George's Park, Wandsworth, conferring with a person of foreign appearance who was later identified as the then Second Secretary of the U.S.S.R. Embassy—and the story of how he came to be in such company is a curious one.

Marshall at the age of fourteen had joined the Sea Cadets. He did not remain a Sea Cadet for very long, but during the short period when he had taken part in their activities he had managed to learn the Morse Code. When he was called up to do his National Service four years later, in 1945, he could still remember the Morse Code, and as a result he was posted in the Royal Corps of Signals and trained as a radio operator. In this capacity his conduct was unremarkable. He did well enough not to attract adverse criticism, saw service in Palestine and Egypt, and, in June 1948, was demobbed.

For a young man whose sole qualification is that he can operate a Morse key, there are several possible careers. He can join the Merchant Navy or the Post Office—or the Diplomatic Wireless Service, the small corps of men which transmits and receives all the highly confidential messages that flash between Her Majesty's government and the various British Embassies throughout the world. The pay is not high—about seven pounds a week, perhaps. But one travels on two-year duty tours, during which time one sees foreign countries and can give one's address to friends as being "care of the British Embassy".

It was the Diplomatic Wireless Service that appealed to Marshall and he spent six months after his demobilization applying in vain to join it. However, he practised sedulously on his Morse key, and finally, in November 1948, he was admitted, at last, and posted for fourteen months to the Middle East. Then, after a brief spell in England, he was sent to Moscow.

Life for an official of the British Embassy in Moscow is often not easy. Particularly it was not easy in 1950, when there was serious tension behind the Iron Curtain. It was very gratifying to Marshall to be sent to Moscow as an employee of the Foreign Office, and his parents were proud of the Russian clock he sent to them, which played the "Harry Lime Theme"; but in the British Embassy itself, Marshall, the wireless operator, was not an exalted personage. The Ambassador and his personal staff—the First, Second, and Third Secretaries—the confidential clerks, *aides* and *attachés*—were responsible diplomats and also men of experience and background. Understandably enough, Marshall did not find himself on intimate terms with them, and it was difficult for him to find companions with tastes similar to his own—which seem to have been restricted to film-going in no very critical spirit, and making silk mats. The lad was in any case rather retiring, and scarcely the type of youth to make friends easily in any circumstances.

To pass his leisure time he used, not surprisingly, to go frequently to the cinema, but as he was in Moscow and no longer in his native Wandsworth—where he had done the same thing—he had difficulty in understanding the dialogue. He therefore decided—very laudably—that he would take Russian lessons to help him get the hang of what was going on in the Russian films.

Thus, presumably, he made some Russian contacts, and after a while he attracted the attention of the Russian Intelligence Service, to whom, no doubt, the lonely boy with time on his hands and no especial interests or status seemed promising material. He was taken in hand, offered social contacts, entertainment, and instruction, and made to feel that he was a person of some importance in Moscow.

In December 1951, however, he was posted back to England, and normally his future contacts with Russians would have been very tenuous. However, in his diary for the month of January 1952 an entry appeared which read: "SE 13 Ken Pal Gdns. 18.16.10." This was later interpreted by M.I.5 security officers as: "Soviet Embassy, 13, Kensington Palace Gardens, also at Nos. 18, 16 and 10;" No. 10 Kensington Palace Gardens is the address of the Soviet Naval Attaché.

Marshall had gone back to routine duties at the Diplomatic Wireless Station in Hanslope Park, Buckinghamshire. One of the first things he did was to attend a meeting of the British-Soviet Friendship Society at Holborn Hall on 12th June. This reminiscent affection might seem quite natural, but on 25th May, just over a fortnight before, he had shown a more suspect hankering for Russian company. He had met by arrangement, a man later identified as Kuznetsov, a Second Secretary at the Soviet Embassy, in Kingston-upon-Thames, and the two had gone for lunch together in the restaurant of Bentall's department store.

One can easily imagine that Marshall was flattered to be taken to lunch by a Second Secretary of an Embassy—any Embassy! The agents of the Intelligence Service of the U.S.S.R. in Britain are usually far too astute to take their contacts to lunch, even in such untoward places as department stores in Kingston-upon-Thames, but it is to be presumed that Kuznetsov knew the psychological value of such an invitation to young Marshall, and considered that the risk was justified by the gain. Actually it was not, but that is by the way. The two men continued to meet at various times. They even had lunch at the Berkeley in Piccadilly, and that was most foolish.

Probably Kuznetsov realized this himself or, more probably, once he had got Marshall into the state of mind where he fancied himself as a romantic figure—a spy—he easily persuaded him to forgo the rewards of lunches for the safer alternative of meeting in King George's Park at Wandsworth.

M.I.5 agents had on several occasions watched them sit together on a bench and engage in earnest talk. Neither man had the slightest suspicion that they were under observation at this time, and it was felt best that they should not be made uneasy by the appearance of any uniformed police officers, so for six weeks the Wandsworth uniformed men were asked to stay away from King George's Park while the investigation proceeded.

On the day that Marshall was arrested he was seen in the morning to go to the park and wander about as if looking for someone. Then he went to Putney and visited two hotels and a café without staying very long. At lunch-time he went home, and at 6.40 p.m. came out again and went to King George's Park. By this time Kuznetsov had his informant well trained. The days of luncheon at the Berkeley were really over. If he wished to keep him waiting all day it was apparent that Marshall spent the day waiting, and there was an end to it.

Eventually, however, the Embassy Secretary arrived and the two men sat together talking on a park bench for about an hour from 7.30 until 8.30 p.m. Then they walked together towards the park exit, and there Chief Inspector Hughes and other officers of Scotland Yard's Special Branch were waiting to arrest them. Marshall went very white, and his companion told the police that he was Pavel Kuznetsov, Second Secretary at the Soviet Embassy, adding: "It is up to you to prove your suspicions." He said no more until they reached Wandsworth Police Station, at which point he produced the inevitable certificate of diplomatic immunity. He was released immediately his identity was established, and Marshall was detained. Marshall watched Kuznetsov go with some dismay.

Kuznetsov's career as a diplomat had been badly damaged, if not finally brought to its end. Whether his masters in the Kremlin would appreciate his past services enough to overlook his present embarrassing blunder he could not, at that moment, know. One can hardly wonder that he did not have time to spare for the miserable boy who stayed behind in the hands of the police, with no certificate of diplomatic immunity to save him from paying the heavy price of his folly.

The same evening, when Chief Inspector Hughes took young Marshall to his home in Elborough Street, Mrs. Marshall came out to greet them warmly. But as she did so her son said: "This is a detective, Mum. I'm under arrest."

Kuznetsov, of course, became *persona non grata* in this country and was obliged to return to Moscow. It may be that some people will consider that a not very satisfactory or dramatic ending to this story. Yet it is by this persistent neutralization of foreign agents that, unostentatiously, the Department achieves its objects. Every foreign agent who has laboriously acquired experience in his work is valuable to the power for which he is working; every agent who is obliged to leave this country represents a loss to that power of a valuable and trained employee.

The way in which Marshall was led to give away secrets to the Russians was somewhat exceptional. There is no evidence that the young man was ever seriously interested in Communism or, indeed, that he had even thought very much about it. His only concern was a rather childish longing to become a story-book—or, probably, a film—hero, playing an exciting, important role in an international spy drama. It is a longing most people can understand and it is probably felt in a vague, passive way by many young men besides Marshall, who are never tempted to have dealings with foreign powers because they do not happen to work in the Diplomatic Wireless Service or in any other capacity to give them access to information which might be useful to a foreign intelligence service.

A most distressing case came to light about the same time that Marshall was committed for trial. A sensitive, intelligent boy named Tony Dewick was called up for military service in March 1952. Before that he had worked at a travel agency in London, and in his leisure hours he had read a certain amount of Communist literature in West End bookshops. As a result he came to think that he would like to become a Communist and joined the young Communist League, which has a membership of about 4,000 young people aged between fourteen and eighteen—ages when it is exciting to belong to an organization which seems to savour of idealism and revolution and membership of which one probably either conceals from (or defiantly flaunts in front of) one's parents! When a Young Communist reaches the age of eighteen—that is, when he is old enough to be called up—his membership is automatically suspended, but the Communist Party makes sure of not losing sight of him. Wherever he happens to be stationed in England, there are Communists who will welcome him for a meal, a drink, or an evening's hospitality, and he is given their addresses by the Party. National Service men are frequently at a loss for something to do and somewhere to go, so it is scarcely surprising if, without necessarily having remained ardent Communist sympathizers, they accept such invitations. And as long as they do, they are to a certain extent still within the Communist fold. As well as this, Communist literature is still sent to erstwhile Young Communists. While Dewick was stationed at Bovington Camp in Dorset he continued to receive by post copies of *Challenge* and other Communist publications. When, later, it was necessary to search his kitbag, many of them were found.

However, during the early days of his National Service, he was believed to have the makings of a good soldier and no one thought more about him than that. The technical adjutant Captain W. F. Cornish of the R.A.C., selected him within two or three days of his arrival at the camp to be his personal assistant.

By what tortuous ways the lad's mind brought him to the decision that it was his duty to pass information to the Communists, one cannot really know. But the fact remains that Dewick conceived it his duty to pass on to the Communist Party such technical secrets as he could obtain as a result of his position as personal clerk to the technical adjutant. Evidence was given that his unit had Centurion, Comet, and Cromwell tanks, and various types of self-propelled guns, including the Valentine and M.10, and that reports were regularly received from Korea concerning the performances under active service conditions of these armaments, and there is no doubt that although Dewick was not in a position to possess himself of vital secrets as did Fuchs and Nunn May, he could have supplied information of considerable interest and value to the Communist forces fighting his own countrymen in Korea. Quite sincerely, in his muddled state of mind, he felt himself justified in doing this because, in his own words: "I wanted to do something for the organization to which I belonged. I thought it was important to be loyal to it."

That he also belonged to the Army, and would have betrayed trust put in him by his Army comrades, did not seem to have occurred to him; nor did he reflect that the information he stood prepared to hand over might well have enabled the Communists in Korea and Malaya to have killed hundreds of British boys just like himself.

From other documents found in his possession it became apparent that he was in touch with numerous other young Communists, and that the removal of his name from the Party list when he joined the Army was a purely routine procedure that did not exclude him from being able to find Communist friends—including girl friends—when he wished.

In actual fact, Dewick never did succeed in passing any information to the Communists, for M.I.5 arranged that he should be arrested whilst on his way to make preliminary arrangements to do so. Mr. Skardon put it to him: "Do you realize that within a month you might have found yourself passing secret information to a foreign power?"

This might well have been his fate if he had not been stopped in time.

I understand that Dewick afterwards promised his mother

he would have nothing more to do with the Communists, and I can only hope that when he came out of prison after serving his twelve months sentence, he felt it as important to keep that promise as he had felt it important to keep faith with his country's enemies.

CHAPTER TWENTY-ONE

Official visits to Commonwealth countries and the United States –
My inspection of the Police Training School at Rome and the Celere
Battalion – I am granted a Special Audience by the Pope.

W HEN I was a lad my one desire had been to travel. Yet
when once I had succeeded in getting myself a job in
Southern Rhodesia I had settled down. I inevitably
saw a great deal of Africa, but when eventually I came back to
England I no longer hankered after other lands. I am, I suppose, rather lazy about travelling, and once I had proved to
myself that I could get myself to another continent if only I
set my mind to it, I ceased to bother any more.

It so happened, however, that eventually my M.I.5 job
thrust travelling upon me. The disclosing of the spy ring in
Canada which immediately preceded my appointment made
the Department much more conscious than it had previously
been of the possibility of security leakages in the Commonwealth countries which share our secrets. And we were becoming ever more aware that among peoples under British
rule who were gradually becoming politically mature and
groping towards self-government, the firebrands and mal-
contents—as well as the men who sincerely felt that Britain
was pursuing an overbearing policy towards them—were
being stirred wherever possible to rebellion and trouble-
making by Communists. For it is the Communist policy to
foment disagreements that might be resolved by good will and
clear thinking until there is so much anger and misunderstand-
ing and exaggeration that the only outcome possible is hatred
and bloodshed. The more trouble that can be made all over the
world for Britain, the less able this country will be to defend
her interests nearer home, and in the Commonwealth and
colonies no less than inside Britain herself, converts to Com-

munism—no matter how muddle-headed—might come in useful if there were war between Russia and Britain.

Thus I received invitations from Commonwealth Governments to pay them a visit so that I could advise them on the spot about problems which might be new to them but of which we in Britain had some experience, and also to discuss difficulties which both our countries were trying simultaneously to surmount.

My first trip of all, in the autumn of 1946, was to Egypt and Palestine, returning by way of Johannesburg—an experience I should have enjoyed better if I had not been put practically out of action by the results of my routine vaccination before my departure! The following year I visited Nairobi and Salisbury in the summer and Canada and the United States some three weeks later. My first major task in the colonies was initiated in 1948, when, after a tremendously interesting, though brief, glimpse of Australia and New Zealand, I made my way by plane to Singapore and Malaya, where I was instrumental in setting up the new Malayan intelligence organization—assisted by Mr. MacDonald of M.I.5, who had worked previously as an officer in the Indian Police and had experience of the ways of Dacoity.

As a result of my visits to police forces in the colonies, I felt it necessary to report that it seemed to me unfortunate and illogical that while there were at that time five Inspectors of Constabulary for Britain, there was nobody at all inspecting and reporting on the police in the colonies. Colonial governors certainly sent in reports of their own, but that had hardly the same effect as a report by an expert in direct touch with conditions on the spot and also with the Colonial Office, whose job it would be to ascertain precisely what measures should be taken in London to ensure first-rate local police efficiency.

In Malaya I stayed with the Governor, then Sir Edward Gent (who was tragically killed in an aeroplane accident shortly afterwards), and at his house in the hills, forty miles from Kuala Lumpur, I was stricken with appendicitis. The experience of being rushed those forty miles by night in great pain to reach Mr. J. A. P. Cameron, a Scottish surgeon, for an immediate operation was not one I should like to repeat, and about this time I began to wonder apprehensively if travel did not seem to be affecting me rather deleteriously. Thanks to penicillin, however, I recovered rapidly.

This was not, incidentally, the first time that I had reason to be grateful to Sir Alexander Fleming, for in 1913, when I returned to England still suffering from the after-effects of malaria and blackwater fever, I was advised to see him—he was then a pathologist at St. Mary's Hospital in London—and to obtain from him injections to clear my blood of the disease. We never entirely lost sight of each other after that, and he was kind enough to spare some time while I was working in Glasgow to make a vaccine for the use of the police surgeon, Dr. Imrie, to assist him in his efforts to counter the appalling epidemics of influenza and the many cases of common colds which were constantly seriously reducing the police strength there.

In the course of my next few years with M.I.5 I made several visits to the United States and Canada, and, in 1951, returned once more to Australia and New Zealand. It is interesting, I think, to note the different security systems operating in Canada, Australia and New Zealand, each one adapted to suit the needs of the country. For instance, the Australian Security and Intelligence Organization which was set up as a result of my 1948 trip (when I had rewarding discussions with the then Prime Minister, the late Mr. Chifley) is a national organization responsible for the whole country and separate—as in Britain—from the various police forces belonging to individual provinces. In New Zealand, however, it was thought best, since the police force itself is a national organization, to leave security measures in the hands of its Special Branch. In Canada, again, security is looked after by the Royal Canadian Mounted Police, which is of course responsible for law enforcement right across Canada. I myself visited outstations in Canada wherever there was a Special Branch Officer, and made my way right across to Vancouver Island. I do not think I have ever enjoyed a business journey so much in my life, and can only hope that the suggestions I was able to make and the discussions in which I took part were of sufficient value to my Canadian colleagues to compensate them for their kindness and hospitality.

I have left until last the occasion of my visit to Kenya with Mr. MacDonald in 1952. I had previously been to Nairobi several times, but in 1952 there was of course a special reason for my trip, as the Mau Mau atrocities had begun to appal us all.

My arrival in Nairobi on 27th November followed on the atrocious butchery which took place in the house of Commander and Mrs. Meiklejohn about seven miles from Thompson's Falls, and I went to inspect the area and to see the actual house where the crime had been committed. The house had been cleaned up to a certain extent, but it was still a most terrible thing to see the traces of the horrors that had taken place there. These two elderly people had been slashed with pangas (chopping knives like wide-bladed swords) until they had both been horribly maimed. Commander Meiklejohn was eventually hacked to death, and his wife received thirty-six vicious gashes, losing an ear and an eye. After my visit to the scene of this crime I hoped most devoutly that my assistance in devising police protection for courageous and helpless people against such barbaric murderers would be of effective use.

Early in December I began my homeward journey. I had arranged with Dollie that I should meet her in Rome so that we might spend Christmas in a hotel at Amalfi. We watched the colourful little processions and listened to the fireworks and the enthusiastic churchbells. Then we went back to Rome to spend the New Year as guests of Sir Gerald Young.

My stay turned out to be unexpectedly interesting, for I was invited by Dr. Pavone, Chief of Police for Italy, to inspect their training schools, and was genuinely impressed by the good discipline and efficiency of these establishments, which are modelled upon the British pattern and were guided in their beginnings by those three great British police officers, Colonel Arthur Young, Colonel Bye, and Colonel Millhouse, with Lieut.-Colonel Pollock attached for a time as resident adviser.

I inspected the Police Training School in Via Guido Reni in Rome, where nine hundred non-commissioned officers and seventy-four police subalterns were under training. We were taken round the whole school and shown the technical and educational classes, physical training, and recreation, and found them of an enviably high standard. In one class seventeen Siamese police officers were undergoing a nine-months' course in warfare against Communist guerillas.

There is a special unit of the Italian security system, known as the Celere Battalion, that is a highly-trained and most efficient mobile column of men whose function is part police and part military, and who are undoubtedly the pick of the Italian troops. They have been trained in commando methods, and are equipped with Fiat jeeps, armoured cars, and motor-cycles.

The standard test required of this Battalion is that it can turn out and be moving off within three minutes of any alarm call, and this was demonstrated for me. Well within the time limit the entire Battalion was under way with sirens screaming. In peacetime their job is to break up demonstrations and to quell riots, and they have been called out four thousand times since 1945.

They are so well respected and feared now by disorderly mobs that it has been many months since they have found it necessary even to draw their truncheons, for the riot fades like magic when the Celere sirens are heard shrieking towards it. The men of the Celere are taught that their job is to cope with trouble swiftly, efficiently, and ruthlessly. Their discipline and air of self-confidence is very impressive indeed. "We are the drawn sword in the hands of law and order," one of their officers told me proudly. And they certainly looked it to me when I was given the great honour of reviewing the full Battalion parade.

It was during this stay in Rome on 3rd January that I was granted a Special Audience by His Holiness the Pope. He gave me a most cordial greeting in slow, clear English, and said: "I know all about you and your responsible duties. You have just come back from Kenya, have you not? I am most anxious to hear from you how things are going out there, and what it is all about, for it seems very disturbing."

I took this opportunity to praise the brave achievements of Bishop Cavallera of the Consolata Mission at Nyeri and the Pope seemed delighted to hear that his bishop had done such excellent work.

I must admit to being extraordinarily impressed by my reception, though neither I nor my wife are Roman Catholics. The Pope had, without doubt, been following the news of events in Kenya with very great attention, and it was obviously out of a desire to document himself further on the situation there that he had intimated he would be willing to receive me. He assured me of the great love he bore for Britain and of his desire to assist her wherever possible.

My wife had instructed me to ask his blessing for ourselves and our two sons, and this he gave me. We have as a remembrance of my visit four small silver medallions which he sent for and presented to me before I left—one for each member of my family.

CHAPTER TWENTY-TWO

My retirement from M.I.5 – I return to South Africa and embark upon my final campaign.

At the end of August 1953 the time came for me to retire from M.I.5. Frankly, I had begun to look forward eagerly to retirement, and the thought of living quietly at Eastbourne with my wife, occupied in writing these memoirs and in taking life very easily indeed, was by no means repugnant to me. For two or three months after leaving M.I.5 nothing happened to interfere with my modest plans. But then, before the end of the year, I was offered another—a most unexpected—task. And now my story—which I had thought to have completed—has a postscript which as yet I can do no more than mention.

I was approached by Sir Ernest Oppenheimer, Chairman of the celebrated De Beers Consolidated Mines and of the Diamond Corporation, with a request. Would I undertake the investigation of the illicit trafficking in diamonds which is now causing the producers to suffer enormous losses?

The job which I was being offered proved an irresistible temptation—of course I could not bring myself to decline it. At the outset of my career I had gone out to Southern Rhodesia as a very ordinary trooper in the British South Africa Police. Cecil Rhodes, the first and most illustrious Chairman of De Beers, had died only six years previously and Rhodesia was a new country whose immense possibilities he had so ably foreseen. The British South Africa Police Force—which was, incidentally, indebted to De Beers for the financial assistance which had made its existence possible in those pioneering days —was a young force with opportunities for a young man. For me, to return to Rhodesia—and other parts of Africa—at the request of De Beers and on an important mission after nearly half a century was a most romantic and nostalgic assignment, as well as being one that promised interest and excitement.

During my early years in the British South Africa Police, I had already become familiar with cases of diamond smuggling. Indeed, theft and smuggling had been discovered only four years after the first African diamond had been found at Hope Town on the Orange River in 1866. A young, unsuccessful prospector saw an opportunity to steal a couple of mail bags from the Dutoitspan post office and to abstract from them parcels of valuable diamonds which his more fortunate fellow diggers were despatching to buyers. Some of them were not even insured! The young man managed to leave the Dutoitspan district without attracting attention to himself and made his way to Cape Town. There he boarded a steamer, but had the misfortune to run into one of his creditors just before he sailed. In his anxiety to appease this man, he offered to pay all his debts with such alacrity that the creditor began to suspect his sudden affluence. He reported his suspicions to the police, the young prospector's belongings were carefully searched, and eventually a small fortune was discovered—stuffed in the barrels of three shot-guns and concealed in the spare spaces of gun-cases. There have, I fear, been many similar incidents in the years which have passed since then and the police have had plenty of opportunities of practising their detective skill in combating the ingenuity with which diamond thieves have sought to smuggle their loot from the country. It is alarming how easily fabulous riches can be hidden when those riches happen to be in the form of the "bright pebbles" of the diamond-bearing soil of Africa.

It was not long before the business of illicit diamond buying was a flourishing one. It was no longer a case of a stray individual here and there succumbing to sudden temptation and stealing on his own account. Now native workers were offered money to steal from their employers' claims and hand the stones over to the illicit diamond buyers (known as I.D.B.s) who were able, of course, to obtain far greater sums when they in their turn sold the diamonds overseas.

African workers were known to swallow stones so that they could steal them; sometimes they concealed diamonds in self-inflicted cuts, binding up the wound with the gem inside (and generally ending up with a festering sore); and every conceivable physical hiding place was utilized.

Before the turn of the century, the police had learned to search the lead of bullets, to watch for small holes cut in the middle pages of books, to find specially contrived cavities in the heels of shoes, or in the tops of walking sticks. Their task was formidable. The stones were so small in bulk that the risk of detection often seemed to the thief to be negligible; and the rewards in terms of wealth for the clever smuggler were colossal. It is small wonder that the numbers of thieves and I.D.B.s have not decreased with the years, despite the measures which have been taken against them.

Recently, particularly since the end of the war, smuggled diamonds have become a sort of international crooks' currency. Adventurers have taken advantage of currency regulations by using smuggled diamonds in place of currency to defeat the ends of the regulations and make a handsome profit for themselves by judicious exporting and importing regardless of trading restrictions.

"Carriers" have been easily found to transport—and smuggle the stones on behalf of the international gangs. Foolish people have been prepared in return for perhaps no more than a few pounds to take diamonds from, say, Britain to the States, or from Belgium to Tangiers and hand them over to a gang's representative. These "carriers" have been pawns in the game of men who do not wish to take risks on their own account but who are making vast sums while the folk they are using are content with comparatively very little—content, that is, until they are caught! Airline stewards have been made use of in this way, weak characters being singled out and suborned.

Other operations around the British coast are known to have been carried out by gangs in high-speed launches equipped with radar to warn the miscreants of the approach of customs or police patrols—evidently the rewards of successful smuggling exceed the expense involved in installing radar and other elaborate equipment on launches.

To put an international gang of crooks out of action, an international security organization is essential, working in close co-operation with the various police forces. However, in this case it seemed to me that the first necessity was to stop the stealing of diamonds at its source—that is, at the mines themselves. My first task was, therefore, to tour the continent of Africa, talking with the special mine police and security officers, discussing problems with the customs authorities and the police in each country. During April of 1954 I visited the Union of South Africa, the Belgian Congo, Angola, Rhodesia, Tanganyika, and Sierra Leone, talking, and listening and, above all, having a good look round.

Security arrangements differ considerably from one country to another and from one mine to another. In South Africa, for instance, where most of the diamonds come from the large mines in the Kimberley area, security measures are strict, certainly so far as the African workers are concerned. The natives live, during the period for which they have contracted to work in the mines, in large compounds rather like army barracks, where all necessities are provided for them. They are not allowed to leave the area of their compound until their employment is finished. In South Africa the contract is usually for four months, but it is often carried on at the man's request to eight months and even longer. The mines do not have to recruit African labour but rely entirely upon volunteers. Large numbers return to the mines year after year. The conditions are excellent and the men are well content with the arrangement—unless, of course, they had been hoping to find opportunities to steal, in which case they are disappointed. When the day comes round for the men to leave (they do not know which day, precisely, this will be), they are subjected to a very thorough examination, including an X-ray, which leaves them no possibility of concealing diamonds either in or about their persons. Yet diamonds still disappear from the South African mines as elsewhere. European workers are not asked to submit to such stringent examination, though they are all liable to search—there seems to me to be little doubt that a few Europeans are themselves guilty of theft and unworthy of the confidence placed in them by their employers.

In the case of the alluvial fields in Sierra Leone there are undoubtedly greater opportunities for dishonesty. There is also room for better security measures generally, however, and I see no reason why matters should not shortly improve.

After my African trip I submitted my report to Sir Ernest Oppenheimer. The story of our struggle against the diamond smugglers is only just beginning and I cannot yet reveal what measures will be taken nor how much we already know. Until the whole tale can be told, my own autobiography will remain in a sense incomplete. It is, I know, unsatisfactory for the reader who, having got this far, will presumably wish to know the end. I can only apologize and trust that one day I may have the privilege of recording all the details of the last campaign in which I shall take part—the campaign of the diamond producers against the big shots of the international diamond-smuggling racket.

INDEX

ABBIS, SIR GEORGE, 86
Abercorn (N. Rhodesia), 30, 31
Aitcheson, Lord, 134, 135
Akers, Sir Wallace, 170–1
Amalfi, 193
Anderson, Sir John (now Viscount Waverley), 171
Anglo-American Oil Company, 8
Anglo-Belge Boundary Commission, 21, 24
Angola, 199
Appleyard, Walter, J.P., 92–3
Ashford (Kent), 152
Atomic secrets, betrayal of, 165–6, 171–4, 177
Attercliffe (Yorks.), 103, 104
Attlee, Rt. Hon. Clement R., on Fuchs case, 176–7
Australia, 191; security system in, 192
Avory, Sir Horace Edmund, 93–4

BANYARUANDA TRIBE, 41–5
Batutsi tribes, 41
Beehive Gang (Glasgow), 124–5
Belgian Congo, 21, 25, 39, 41, 199
Beresford, Tristan, Q.C., 55, 57–8
Berrett, Chief Detective-Inspector, 98, 101
Bevan, Stuart, K.C., 93
Beverley (Yorks.), 51, 52
Billericay, 99–100
Billy Boys Gang (Glasgow), 127–33
Bismarkburg Province (German East Africa), 32
Blanch Farm Gate incident, 52–8
Bodle, Colonel Billy, 11
Bowman, "Bull" (Glasgow gangster), 128

British South Africa Police, 8–39, 197; Sillitoe joins, 8–9; discipline in, 10, 13; Askaris in, 20, 31; Sillitoe resigns, 39
British-Soviet Friendship Society, 184
Broken Hill (N. Rhodesia), 30
Browne, Frederick Guy, and Gutteridge murder, 98–106
Bruce, Sir Robert, 112
Bulawayo, 11, 12, 14, 15, 18
Burgess, Edward, 72
Bye, Colonel, 193

CAMERON, J. A. P., 191
Campbell, Bailie Hugh, 116–18, 120
Canada, 169, 173, 191; spy ring in, 190; security system, 192
"Cape to Cairo Motor Expedition" (1914), 27–8
Cargill, Sir John, 107–8
Carson, John, 144
Cassels, Sir James Dale, 92, 93
Cavallera, Bishop, 195
Celere Battalion (Rome), 194
Central Africa, 32–9, 40–7
Chapman, Jim, 12
Chartwell, 156–7
Chesterfield: Sillitoe as Chief Constable of, 50–2, 58, 77; Dr. J. M. Webster at, 69–70
Chicago, 110
Chifley, Rt. Hon. J. B., 192
Christ's Hospital, 2
Churchill, Rt. Hon. Sir Winston S., 155–7
"Cinema Bandit," 140–2
City Imperial Volunteers, 7, 39